DANVILLE PUBLIC LIBRARY

3 1205 00174 8506

C0-ATY-199

WITHDRAWN

261.1097 Evans, Anthony T.
EVA          America's only hope.

$14.95

| DATE | | | |
|---|---|---|---|
|  |  |  |  |
|  |  |  |  |
|  |  |  |  |
|  |  |  |  |
|  |  |  |  |
|  |  |  |  |
|  |  |  |  |
|  |  |  |  |
|  |  |  |  |
|  |  |  |  |
|  |  |  |  |
|  |  |  |  |

9/91

Danville Public Library
Danville, Illinois

PUBLIC LIBRARY
DANVILLE, ILLINOIS
© THE BAKER & TAYLOR CO.

# AMERICA'S
# ONLY HOPE

# AMERICA'S ONLY HOPE

# ANTHONY T. EVANS

**MOODY PRESS**

CHICAGO

## Dedication

*To the wonderful staff leadership
and membership of Oak Cliff Bible Fellowship,
who provide the living context
through which the principles
of this book are modeled.*

---

© 1990 by
ANTHONY T. EVANS

All rights reserved. No part of this book may be reproduced in any form without permission in writing from the publisher, except in the case of brief quotations embodied in critical articles or reviews.

All Scripture quotations, unless noted otherwise, are from the *New American Standard Bible,* © 1960, 1963, 1968, 1971, 1972, 1973, 1975, and 1977 by The Lockman Foundation, and are used by permission.

The use of selected references from various versions of the Bible in this publication does not necessarily imply publisher endorsement of the versions in their entirety.

ISBN: 0-8024-0741-2

1 2 3 4 5 6 Printing/AK/Year 94 93 92 91 90

*Printed in the United States of America*

61.1097
EVA
cop 1

# Contents

Danville Public Library
Danville, Illinois

# Acknowledgments

I want to thank Annie Roberson, my administrative assistant, and those transcribers who worked so closely with her in the preparation of the manuscript. I am also thankful for my wife, Lois, who supported me throughout the preparation of this project. Finally, my appreciation goes to the executive team of Oak Cliff Bible Fellowship—Rev. Martin Hawkins, Rev. Larry Mercer, Rev. Warren Mattox, and Mrs. Ophelia Greene—who served as sounding boards for the ideas in this book and who oversee their implementation in our church.

# Preface

This book was born out of a twofold burden: a burden for my country and a burden for the church. I love America, and I am proud to be an "African" American. In spite of the many problems that have existed, and still exist, in our country, there is no place I would rather live and raise a family than in the United States of America.

Yet our nation suffers from a serious malady. The heart of our nation is diseased by a moral and ethical virus that is spreading rapidly throughout our entire population. This disease of the soul threatens to deliver a national deathblow. Even worse, the disease is not being diagnosed for what it is. We are allocating a great deal of time and money in an attempt to cure the symptoms of the disease, but we have little understanding of the nature of the disease itself. As I observe the multifaceted crisis we face, it is apparent that unless we bring about a major reversal of our moral and ethical frame of reference, we will self-destruct. We are in grave danger of doing to ourselves what no other enemy could do.

Reviewing our history as a nation, I see how the church helped shape our national consciousness and established the framework for our constitution and personal freedoms. By contrast, the church today has an almost invisible impact on our contemporary situation. This change brings me deep concern.

How is it possible for the number of churches in our nation to be increasing while the social impact of the church decreases? Why does the church merely react to society's agenda rather than setting an agenda for society to follow? Why do our political and social leaders not look to the church for answers to the perplexing problems that undermine the very fabric of our society? I can only conclude that the church, for the most part, has stopped being the church.  The church has failed to stand up and be counted.

My hope is that this book will awaken those who read it to the spiritual disease now plaguing our nation and that it will simultaneously awaken the church to its responsibility as our nation's attending physician.  My hope is that the church will provide the antibodies necessary to stop the disease and nurse our nation back to spiritual and moral health.  For therein lies *America's Only Hope*.

# Part 1
# The Problem

# 1

## Symptoms of a Sick Society

Humpty Dumpty sat on a wall.
Humpty Dumpty had a great fall.
All the king's horses,
And all the king's men,
Couldn't put Humpty Dumpty together again.

This simple nursery rhyme perfectly illustrates the state of our world and culture today. Mr. Dumpty had firm control of his life; things were going well. But one day, as he walked down the street, he decided to climb a wall and see the world around him. Being a self-sufficient fellow, he climbed the wall all by himself. But while he was up there, something happened, something cataclysmic. We don't know exactly what, but it sent Mr. Dumpty tumbling to the ground. Suddenly he wasn't the man he used to be. He lay on the concrete, shattered into a hundred pieces.

Unable to resolve his crisis, Mr. Dumpty desperately needed help. But notice where that help came from. It didn't come from his family. It didn't come from his job. It didn't come from his friends. It didn't come from his neighbors. Instead, it came from the king—straight from Washington, D.C. But *all* the king's horses and *all* the king's men couldn't do a thing for Mr. Dumpty.

This nursery rhyme has an intriguing twist; it really isn't about Mr. Dumpty at all. It's about all the king's horses and all the king's men. You see, the king and his men jumped right in to help Mr. Dumpty. It was as if the White House called an emergency session of Congress, which passed a law that was supposed to solve the problem. The problem must have been a whopper, because all the members of Congress hopped on their horses (which means their Mercedes and Lincoln Continentals) to solve Mr. Dumpty's tragedy.

However, things did not end well for Mr. Dumpty. All the king's horses and all the king's men could not put him back together. The tragedy is not that Humpty Dumpty is in pieces; the tragedy is that all the king's horses and all the king's men are just as broken as Humpty Dumpty. The tragedy is that Mr. Dumpty put his hope in the government—the best of the land—and it couldn't help him.

We live in a world just like Humpty Dumpty's world. Humpty Dumpty problem solvers offer solutions to our most desperate problems, and when they are done, they have often left nothing but a Humpty Dumpty mess. The tragedy is that those in whom we place confidence to fix our problems are often just as broken as what they are trying to fix.

This truth was displayed in graphic fashion at a special town meeting regarding the drug problems in Washington, D.C., on Ted Koppel's *Nightline*. In a town-meeting format, leaders from Capitol Hill, representatives from the President's staff, community leaders, and concerned citizens discussed the siege that city is under due to crime and drugs. Hour after hour, some of the king's men and some of the hurting people talked, proposed, and accused. When it was over, they were no closer to solving the problem than when they began.

Meanwhile, the problems of our society desperately need help. From inner-city drug lords to homosexuals in Congress to "inside" traders on Wall Street to fraudulent abusers (on both the giving and receiving ends) of the welfare system, it is clear that a moral crisis affects all levels of our society. We must be careful not to think of this moral crisis as an "inner city" or "minority" problem, for it crosses all racial and class lines. A look at some of the problems we face will help us understand the breadth and depth of our society's deterioration.

## POVERTY

In 1964, under the banner of President Johnson's "Great Society," all the king's men decided to eliminate poverty by declaring war on it. What a well-financed war it has been: beginning with $2 billion in 1964 and soaring to $180 billion fifteen years later, the government spent more than $1 trillion to lift the poor out of poverty. What a well-equipped war it has been: it created more than 100 social service agencies that employed 1 out of every 100 American workers.[1]

But we are losing this war, and losing it big. Twenty-five years later, 1 out of every 4 American children lives in poverty. The elderly account for 35 percent of the poor.[2] And the greatest losers are women, who now make up 77 percent of this country's poor.[3]

The devastating effects of this war are far-reaching. From a purely economic standpoint, the effort is a tragic failure; 70 percent of the allocated funds have gone to the middle-class administrators of the program, leaving only 30 percent for those in need.[4]

On a personal level, it is even worse. The welfare system designed to help the poor has in reality helped to destroy them. It has killed their initiative. Welfare itself has become like a drug that gives a quick fix but in the long run destroys. Today we not only face a huge price tag—an expected $21 billion for welfare in 1992—but have the burden of repairing the lives that welfare has destroyed.[5]

Certainly there have been private attempts to do something about this problem. We have had band-aid, farm-aid, live-aid, fashion-aid, and AIDS-aid. We have seen hands stretched across America. We've heard songs like "We Are the World" that raised millions of dollars. Yet when it's all done, the celebrity industry is the winner. A few million dollars have been raised, but the poor keep getting poorer.

In some cases, a plea for "helping the poor" has been turned into a way to satisfy the passion for materialism. Atlantic City, New Jersey, for instance, became a gambling center because its promoters promised to revitalize the area with gambling revenues. But that hasn't happened. Atlantic City now has the highest crime rate in the state. Gambling proceeds are $2.73 billion a year,[6] but local rescue missions are filled to overflowing. Instead of saving the city, the promoters are destroying it while they add to their riches.

We also see the effects of poverty in a growing homeless population. An estimated 3 million homeless people try to make do with only 100,000 available beds.[7] The problem is dramatically portrayed at night on Pennsylvania Avenue in Washington, D.C. On one side of the street, bright lights illuminate the White House—the power center of our nation. On the other side of the street, in the shadows, sit the homeless—the helpless who have no place to go.

Accompanying this catastrophe is the greediness of some who have been entrusted with the welfare of the poor. When the books are opened, scandal after scandal like those in HUD has skimmed off millions of dollars intended for the homeless.

Why has all of this happened? Why did things get even worse after the war on poverty was declared? It happened because the king, his men, and the broken people didn't understand that good intentions do not necessarily make good social policy.

## RACIAL AND CLASS CONFLICT

In addition to the seemingly irreparable problem of poverty, we find ourselves entangled in a never-ceasing racial and class crisis. This country has failed to come to grips with the color line. Racial fires burn from Howard Beach, New York, to Miami and beyond. As we face increasing budgetary restraints, class conflict will escalate. The middle class, which wants to support the existing infrastructure and promote business development, is on a collision course with the lower class that suffers in poverty.

These struggles even occur across class lines within the minority community. Tension is building between the black middle class and the black lower class. The black middle class has increasingly moved to suburbia, leaving the black lower class without encouraging role models or economic potential. Historically, the black middle class has provided such models and potential. Now the absence of middle-class blacks creates further hopelessness and despair among the black lower class and fosters tension between brothers and sisters.

Many had hoped that Uncle Sam had resolved the problem of racial discrimination through the passage of civil rights legislation. However, despite the Civil Rights Act, the Equal Employment Opportunity Commission, and the election of minority representatives to major local and national posts throughout this nation, racial tension is growing again at an alarming rate. The Ku Klux Klan and neo-Nazi groups are attempting a resurgence, while the NAACP and The Urban League are continually having to combat racial discrimination. It is evident that changed laws do not change hearts.

## DISEASE

Disease, AIDS in particular, is another crisis that we can't begin to fix. The medical world feverishly searches for a cure, but by 1991 an estimated 400,000 people will be dead or dying from AIDS. Another 15 million people will also be infected by the virus. By 1992, we will be out of hospital beds to handle AIDS cases.[8]

The costs associated with treating this disease are staggering. Conservatively, it takes $75,000 to treat—not cure—each case, which will require an expenditure of more than $30 billion over the next few years.[9]

The black community is being devastated by this disease. Blacks make up only 12 percent of the general population but account for 25 percent of all AIDS cases. A horrifying 50 percent of all children born with AIDS are black.[10]

Despite this calamity, homosexuals demand freedoms that would never be granted to people who suffer from other deadly communicable diseases. Yet the homosexual lobby is a political force to be reckoned with in America today.

## BROKEN FAMILIES

After twenty years of failed social programs, the once-stable institution of the American family is rapidly deteriorating. No-fault divorce has made it easy to tear apart the family structure, which is the hub of any society. Currently, 50 percent of all marriages in this country end in divorce. Many of the remaining couples stay together because of finances or only for the sake of their children.

In the inner city, the disintegration of the family is even greater. Six out of ten black children grow up without a father.[11] More black men are in prison than in college. Two-parent families are now the exception in the inner city; by the year 2000, only one in five black babies will be born to two-parent families.[12] The Children Defense Fund discovered that 90 percent of all babies born to black teenage mothers are born outside of marriage.

The increasing dehumanization of women through pornography and the celebration of violence depicted on television and in movies adds fuel to the family crisis. In such an environment, it is no wonder that the incidents of child abuse, wife beating, and rape are soaring. Such crimes devastate the family structure.

The increase of gangs in our cities—and, yes, even in our suburbs—is directly related to the family breakdown. Gangs are actually alternative families. Many kids don't find self-esteem, respect, or dignity in their nuclear family. And because they are human, they desperately need self-worth. So they find it in another family—the gang. Gangs do many bad things, but they also let kids know that they are somebody. When you run with a gang, you have an identity, you have power, you have a reputation, you have significance, and you have prestige. That's why gangs are so appealing.

The breakdown of the family has also led to an educational breakdown. Teachers must now do much more than teach. They serve as social workers for children from broken homes. Sometimes they function more like police officers than teachers when dealing with rebellious children. And with increasing violence in our schools, teachers at times need police protection from their students.

## HOPELESS YOUNG PEOPLE

The disintegration of the family has also contributed to an overwhelming feeling of hopelessness among our young people. Adolescents attempt suicide 400,000 times each year, and 6,500 of them succeed.[13] What makes more than 1,000 young people in the prime of life want to die each day?

There's a story about a father who told his son, "I want you to get a good education."

"Why, Dad?" the son asked.

"So you can get a good job, live in a good neighborhood, wear good clothes, and drive a good car," the father replied.

"But, Dad, why do I want to do that?"

"So you can raise your family and send your kids to college so they can get good jobs and live in nice neighborhoods."

"But, Dad," the son insisted, "what's the point of doing all that?"

Finally the exasperated father said, "So you can retire with dignity and die and have something to leave behind!"

Many of our young people are like this son. They see no point in living life as their parents have lived it. Even those of the middle and upper classes have lost purpose. They have lost all hope. They find the potential of death more appealing than the reality of life.

If they don't choose death, they may live out their emptiness in other destructive ways. The graphic illustration of this is the "wilding" incident in Central Park, New York, in which a gang of kids brutally beat and raped a jogger. "Wilding" is nothing new. When I was young, it meant writing graffiti or breaking windows. But now young people are turned on by violence, destruction, and death. Even kids from nice neighborhoods combat the emptiness of life with thrilling experiences—the more violent and bizarre the better.

## ABORTION

Abortion is America's new, big-money business. It is the process of committing first-degree murder in the name of convenience and profit. Each year more than 1.5 million unborn babies are intentionally murdered. That is more than 4,000 babies poisoned, chopped up, suctioned out, and left to die every day. Since 1973, more than 23 million unborn children have been slaughtered for convenience.[14]

Abortion has been particularly destructive to the minority community, since one-third to one-half of all abortions in the United States are performed on minority women. For every black baby born, two are aborted.[15]

Planned Parenthood is an intentional part of this murderous process. Seventy percent of all their clinics are strategically placed in black or hispanic neighborhoods. Planned Parenthood offers school-based clinics (primarily in minority neighborhoods), but they do not offer morality. After all their sex education, we do not see decreasing immorality. Instead, we see increased promiscuity, pregnancy, and high-risk sexual behavior. In 1980, when there was much less sex education, 4 million cases of venereal disease were reported among adolescents and young adults. Now 14 million cases surface every year.[16] In addition, teenage pregnancy is completely out of hand, and no one has a solution.

## CRIME AND DRUGS

As bad as the aforementioned problems are, our nation's greatest burden is the epidemic of crime and its unique relationship to drugs. The situation in Washington, D.C., shows just how serious the problem is. There, murder has become the norm. Seventy-two percent of homicide victims are between the ages of eighteen and thirty-nine, and 90 percent of them are black. Of those who commit crimes, 63 percent have dope or alcohol in their systems at the time.[17]

Many big-city leaders believe the crime/drug problem is virtually impossible to overcome. Crime and drugs have outstripped the ability of government agencies, police departments, courts, and prisons to handle the problem. Meanwhile, the drug lords face no budget crisis. They have an ever-increasing flow of resources to keep their enterprises functioning and growing. In utter hopelessness, some politicians are even suggesting that we legalize drugs. In effect they are saying they have no answers and are ready to give up.

But legalization is not the answer. The increasing number of addicts and the increasingly devastating effects of new drugs, such as "ice," will only create a new set of strains on our society. We will have to finance already skyrocketing health care costs to care for these new addicts.

Due to the pressure of increasing numbers of criminals, which is in part due to the drug crisis, our prison system is like a revolving door. Those who are imprisoned are merely released again. Even so, our prison population grows by 900 inmates a week.[18] At this rate, we cannot keep up with the demand. By the time new prisons are built, they are inadequate.

The random violence that accompanies drug activity keeps law-abiding, inner-city citizens living—and raising their children—in fear. In some places citizens have taken matters into their own hands, establishing patrols and barricades to protect their neighborhoods. Even the church is no longer protected from crime. Recently our assistant pastor and three women in our church were held at gunpoint while thieves took what they wanted to finance their drug habits. The police publicly acknowledge that they can't solve the problem. As one policeman commented, "We have now moved to the level of lawlessness."

I have seen the reality of such lawlessness even in the inner-city neighborhood where I was raised. Each summer I take my children to see their grandparents, who still live in Baltimore, Maryland. Each summer we get a new lesson in urban crime, violence, and drugs. During our last visit, we sat on the front porch and watched as the people next door served crack to the never-ending traffic of poor-, middle-, and upper-class customers. We saw young kids deliver crack to customers. We saw lookouts sit in their cars and honk the horn if danger appeared. We watched policemen chase down teenage drug addicts. And we were watched. One night my father's car was destroyed to serve notice that we'd better mind our own business.

What my family and I witnessed in Baltimore was a tightly knit web of economic development and criminal behavior converge at the same time. Crack is the new king in almost every urban center in this country. How can you tell a teenager who has no hope, no direction, and no father that he should flip hamburgers for $4.25 an hour when he can make $500 to $1,000 a week working for the local drug kingpin?

The drug lords who prey on the inner cities are fed by a massive, middle-class clientele that hides its addictions behind pin-striped suits. Seventy-six percent of illegal drug use in our country is among whites, who pump profits into the drug lords' pockets and keep drugs flowing into our inner cities. President Bush has offered $7.8 billion to solve the problem, but without a solution to user demand, there is no solution. Humpty Dumpty still needs help.

Despite the valiant efforts of sincere, caring people who serve in many community programs that have addressed these issues with some success, the problems of our society grow worse. The reason is that the problems are only symptoms of a spiritual and moral disease. Until we effectively deal with the root cause of the problems, we cannot solve them. Sincerity and helpful programs, although vital, are not sufficient to stop our downward spiral. *Only a spiritual reformation led by the church on the basis of biblical authority can save our nation from its moral decay.* Therein lies America's only hope.

## NOTES

1. Statistic cited by Bob Woodson, president of the National Center for Neighborhood Enterprise, Washington, D.C. This agrees with the statistical data of Charles Murray, *Losing Ground* (New York: Basic Books, 1984), p. 242.
2. George Grant, *Bring in the Sheaves* (Atlanta: American Vision, 1985), p. 35.
3. Julia Wittleson, *The Feminization of Poverty* (Boston: Holy Cross, 1983), p. 19.
4. Cited by Woodson and Murray.
5. *U.S. News and World Report*, 27 November 1989, p. 31.
6. "Boardwalk of Broken Dreams," *Time*, 25 September 1989, pp. 64-69.
7. *Newsweek*, 16 December 1985, pp 22-23.
8. David Chelton, *Power in the Blood* (Brentwood, Tenn.: Wolgemuth and Hyatt, 1987), pp. 22-24.
9. Ibid., p. 22.
10. "AIDS Rate Among Minorities Noted," *Dallas Morning News*, 27 March 1987, p. 35A.
11. *Black News Digest*, U.S. Department of Labor, 13 February 1989.
12. Ibid.
13. J. Kerby Anderson, "Teenage Suicide," *Moody Monthly* 87 (February 1987): 19-21.
14. For an exhaustive discussion of abortion, see George Grant, *Grand Illusions* (Brentwood, Tenn.: Wolgemuth & Hyatt, 1988).
15. Grant, p. 95.
16. Ibid., p. 117.
17. *U.S. News and World Report*, 10 April 1989, pp. 20 ff.
18. Ibid.

# 2

# The Invisible Enemy

If I were a politician, I'd talk about donkeys and elephants and how we need more programs and money to help the poor. If I were a lawyer, I'd talk about laws and why the little man on the street seems to need to break laws in order to survive. If I were an economist, I'd talk about how our gross national product should be sufficient to provide everything we need, especially if we eliminated the federal deficit. But I'm not a politician, a lawyer, or an economist. I am a minister. As a minister, I have a different point of view about Mr. Dumpty's dilemma.

The king's horses and the king's men can't fix Mr. Dumpty because they have little understanding of why he's broken. As a result, they try to resolve Mr. Dumpty's problem without understanding what's really wrong. That's about as helpful as putting Band-Aids® on cancer. So the question we must ask is, "What is the real problem?"

## THE REAL PROBLEM

Simply stated, our nation has lost its moral frame of reference. Every problem mentioned in the previous chapter has its roots in our nation's moral and spiritual breakdown. As our society has dismissed an absolute, God-based, value system from its conscience, we have reaped gloom, doom, and despair. And things will only get worse. As humanism and its New Age cousin increase their dominance in society, devastating social, political, economic, and moral consequences will result. By allowing our traditional, Judeo-Christian frame of reference to erode and by excluding any mention of the divine from our schools, laws, homes, and—yes, even churches—we have delivered our future to the consequences of godlessness.

The fundamental truth that our society has ignored is that every phys-ical problem has a spiritual cause (Ephesians 2:2; 6:12). We think that what we see is all there is. But that is not how God made the universe to work. The Bible explains that the world operates in the physical—what we see, taste, touch, smell, and hear—but that the physical proceeds from the spiritual (Genesis 1:1; Colossians 1:15-16). So the visible actions of individuals, families, and political systems directly result from spiritual stan-dards (Daniel 10:10-21).

Thus, the degradation of our youth is directly related to the lack of their parents' moral code. The corruption of our politicians is due to the fact that money is more important than morality. The epidemic of drug abuse is due to the fact that when greed and fleshly lust mix, they yield decadence. The American family is breaking up because marriage has become a social convenience rather than a divine institution.

It is not mere "bad luck" that causes an even worse problem to occur just as society seems to resolve an existing one. For instance, we first dealt with marijuana, then cocaine. As soon as we recognized the hideousness of cocaine addiction, we had to deal with "crack"—cocaine's cheaper, more deadly, and usually immediately addictive cousin. The latest in this string of problems is "ice," which makes its users more violent than any drug we have known before. So things are getting worse. Sinners are becoming more adept at sinning. This happens for two reasons.

First, there is a spiritual resistance to every step of progress society seeks to make. That resistance—Satan—is determined to keep society deceived and in despair (John 10:10; 1 John 2:15-17; Revelation 20:3).

Second, our problems are getting worse because, for the most part, the church has failed to be the church (Matthew 5:13; 16:18; 1 Peter 4:17). The world, as we've seen, has no idea how to fix Mr. Dumpty. It doesn't even know what's wrong. However, the church—the one and only force in society that can fix Mr. Dumpty—has forgotten that it has been given victory over Satan's evil empire. Until the church decides to be the church God intends it to be, our society will continue its hopeless decline. Mr. Dumpty will remain broken.

As bleak as our society's future may seem, this book is built on the premise that a real solution exists. The church can fix Mr. Dumpty. We can stem the tide of decline that floods our country. Some churches are already doing an excellent job in this area. However, it will take a revival of the whole church—a revival of churches in communities throughout our nation to fix Mr. Dumpty. When Christ returns to set up His kingdom, He will provide ultimate deliverance for society. In the meantime He has delivered His people from the grip of sin. When those people model Christ in every aspect of life, the church will make a powerful impact on society.

## WE'RE FIGHTING A WAR

As we try to deal with the great problems in our society, it should become apparent that we face an all-out war. There are no easy, Band-Aid® solutions to drug abuse, unemployment, prejudice, or poverty. If we are to defeat these destructive problems, we must be prepared to fight. And we must do battle mightily.

This fact should not surprise those of us who call ourselves Christians. The most fundamental issue believers must understand is that, because we have aligned ourselves with God, we are fighting a war against the evil one. Whether we know it or not, we are fighting a war. And we had better be ready to fight.

This war is unique. It is a *spiritual* war, yet it is fought in the *physical* realm. Although we fight the real flesh and blood problems of poverty, drugs, and crime, we cannot fight from a purely physical frame of reference. We must remember that every physical problem has a spiritual cause.

The physical problems we see are merely expressions or symptoms of spiritual issues. Just as an undetected virus or bacteria can destroy the human body, undetected spiritual causes can bring destruction to society. Only by dealing with the underlying cause of sickness can we deal with the symptoms. Thus, we need to understand the root spiritual issues behind the physical problems. If we attempt to solve a problem without understanding the spiritual cause, and thereby finding a spiritual solution, we cannot achieve a long-term solution.

## WHAT'S THE WAR ALL ABOUT?

The war began long before you or I were born. It even began before God created Adam and Eve. We don't know the exact time, but we know the event. It began when Lucifer, the archangel of heaven—whom we call Satan—led a rebellion against God's sovereign rule. We can read about this rebellion in Isaiah 14 and Ezekiel 28. Under Satan's leadership, a group of angels attempted to overthrow, or at least share, God's rule over the universe.

That event changed history because God will not share His glory (Isaiah 42:8). The Bible tells us that God will not share what belongs to Him. He is jealous for what He owns (Exodus 20:5), and He owns everything.

Since He is the owner of the world and all who live in it, His jealousy is legitimate. In a similar way, I am jealous for my wife because she is *my* wife. I am jealous for my home because it is *mine.* So God, the creator of the universe, reserves for Himself the sole right to rule His universe.

When Satan challenged that right and tried to share in God's rule, God kicked him, and all who followed him, out of heaven. Yet Satan did not quit when he was kicked out. Even to this day, he persists in trying to snatch away that which legitimately belongs to God. Even to this day, Satan seeks to grab men out from under God's authority and into his control. His agenda is to get people to rebel against God. That is why we are at war. Satan is still rebelling against God, and we are the territory he seeks to control.

All of human history centers on Satan's rebellion against God. Thus, the great issue for each individual is under whose authority he will place himself. "Will I submit to God as Lord of my life, or will I submit to Satan?" That's the basic question every person must answer.

God has not made us robots who automatically serve Him faithfully. He created us in His image and desires that we promote His image throughout the earth. However, He created us—just as He created the angels—with the power to make moral decisions. God is not interested in mandatory control of our lives. He desires that we *choose* to serve Him.

Satan knows—even before we do—that we have to choose between serving God and serving him. Satan knows that as soon as we rebel against God we automatically come under his authority. As leader of all rebellion against God, Satan desperately wants us on his side.

When we study Satan's first conversation with a human being (Genesis 3:1-5), it becomes clear that God is the key issue. When Satan approached Eve, he didn't talk about shopping, groceries, money, or health. He talked about God. Although Satan convinced Eve to eat the fruit she wasn't supposed to eat, the issue wasn't fruit. The issue was, Who will you obey? So when Eve bit into that fruit, she was saying in essence, "Satan, you are lord of my life. I submit to your authority. You are my god! I will follow your lead. I and my family belong to you." That was exactly what Satan wanted.

Adam and Eve's rebellion had social, economic, and physical consequences. Their rebellion led to the murder of one son by the other. Their rebellion led to a marriage crisis. Their rebellion led to a life in the wilderness rather than in the Garden. Each of these problems resulted from a spiritual root—the decision of Adam and Eve to serve Satan rather than God.

Satan isn't after just one person. His scheme is much greater than that. He wants to control and destroy the human race. That's why he didn't bother Adam until he was married. When he gained control of Adam and Eve, he automatically gained control of their children. That's why Cain killed Abel. In fact, Satan's control increased from generation to generation until the world was so deeply into despair, sin, degradation, and misery that God had to kill the entire population except for Noah and his family (Genesis 6).

Satan is at war with God. He will bring as many people as possible under his control—even if it means destroying all of humanity. The present destruction of humanity in our culture is terrible. Of course we want to do something about it. Yet we must never forget that what we see is only the physical expression of the great spiritual war that surrounds us.

## IF GOD IS GOD, WHY DOESN'T HE JUST END THE WAR?

When we begin to understand the brutal reality of Satan's rebellion against God, one question always comes up: Why, if God is all powerful and sovereign, does He allow the battle to go on? If God is totally in control, why doesn't He just snuff out Satan and end the war? That is a great theological question, and I have a fairly simple answer for it.

I believe that God is only going to go through this kind of challenge one time. He will allow Satan to try everything possible so that no one will ever again think about rebelling against God. I also believe God is giving every man, woman, and young person the opportunity to choose whom he or she will serve.

We see this choice being made repeatedly throughout the Bible. For example, Job had to choose whether to curse God and serve Satan or to stand with God. Over and over again, the children of Israel had to choose between obeying God and worshiping the gods of Satan (Exodus 34:12-17; Deuteronomy 8:19-20; Joshua 24:15). Even Jesus had to choose whether to obey God's Word or follow Satan's enticements. Today, each of us must choose whether to accept Christ as Savior and come under God's authority or whether to accept Satan's lordship.

## WE MUST FIGHT THE REAL WAR

When Adam and Eve bit into the forbidden fruit in the Garden of Eden, Satan took the human race away from God. But when we submit to the lordship of Christ in our lives, we reverse what happened in the Garden. We abandon Satan's rebellion and join God's side. When we change sides, we become a problem to Satan. When we commit our lives to Jesus, not only does Satan lose us, he may lose everything we touch.

For instance, if you are a godly husband, Satan may lose your off-spring. If you are an effective witness, Satan may lose some of your friends and neighbors. You may cause Satan to lose far more than just one person. You may interrupt his program. So Satan will try the same thing with you that he tried in the Garden of Eden. He will try to cut you off at the pass. He will do anything to keep you from helping the other team win. He has to stop you from messing up his diabolical plans.

It isn't exactly encouraging to realize that when we seek to be effective Christians, we take our place on the bloodiest battlefield of the greatest war in history. God is saying, "Follow me. Reflect my image, and expand my kingdom."

Satan says, "No way. I'm going to stop you. I will cause so much pain in your family that you'll forget about God. I'll cause you to be so successful that you'll ignore God's kingdom. I'll keep you so busy or so tired that you can't pursue God's kingdom. I'll keep you so entertained with television programs that you won't bother to pursue His kingdom. Whatever I have to do to keep you from living under God's control and making an impact on the world, I will do it. If there's any way I can get you to pray to me and seek my agenda, I will do it!"

There's no doubt about it, we are fighting a war. The previous chapter described the miserable casualties this war produces. It described the utter futility of our human efforts to win the war. But there's more to the war than meets the eye.

We must not confuse the real war with its casualties. The real war is a spiritual war—the forces of Satan rebelling against God's legitimate, sovereign rule. Ephesians 6:10-13 describes the real war:

> Finally, be strong in the Lord, and in the strength of His might. Put on the full armor of God, that you may be able to stand firm against the schemes of the devil. For our struggle is not against flesh and blood, but against the rulers, against the powers, against the world forces of this darkness, against the spiritual forces of wickedness in the heavenly places. Therefore, take up the full armor of God that you may be able to resist.

Paul knew that the real battle is against Satan. So he makes clear that the battle isn't against flesh and blood—that means against people. He exhorts us to fight the real battle—the spiritual battle. If we are fighting against people, we're not fighting the real battle. If we let Satan dupe us into thinking that our spouses, our children, our neighbors, our bosses, or our friends are the real problem, then he has tricked us. We may fight and fight, but it's for nothing because we never focus on Satan, the real enemy. So we never interface with him, and we never put on the armor of God to fight him.

Satan knows that if he can keep the armor of God off us, we'll never win. So he keeps us confused—rubbing against each other, criticizing one another, and fighting each other. We never ask the vital question: Who is behind all this? But the moment we realize who the real enemy is, we can begin to fight effectively.

Not one of us can go one-on-one with Satan and win. But when we put on God's armor, we can fight and be assured of victory. The outcome of this great war has already been determined. God has already defeated Satan at Calvary. But Satan doesn't want to accept defeat. He is still hiding behind parked cars and sniping at God's army, the church.

Those of us who are Christians have been called to occupy God's territory, to stand firm and fight the real enemy. If we are to stand on the front lines and fight the battle, we must clearly understand the spiritual nature of what we are doing. We must understand that nothing physical exists without a spiritual cause. The challenge is not only to see what we see but to understand what we *can't* see. The moment we understand what we cannot see, we will know how to deal with what we can see. When we understand the spiritual reality behind the physical, we realize that the real battle is spiritual. Then, as spiritual people with spiritual power, we can fight to win.

# 3

# The Enemy's Strategy

Since the issues of our day are primarily spiritual and moral in nature, we must analyze the spiritual strategies being used to bring about our society's destruction. We can develop an antidote for the problems we face only through an adequate spiritual understanding of the problem. In the same way a scientist must identify the nature and process of bacterial infection to develop the right antibacterial agent, the church must understand the enemy and his battle plan. Only then will we be able to overcome the enemy and his destructive forces.

The overriding truth we must recognize is that we are fighting a spiritual war. Ephesians 6:12 describes that war: "our struggle is not against flesh and blood. . . ." In fact, the war is against Satan and his forces—both divine and human. If we are to fight the war successfully, we've got to understand who we are fighting against and how that enemy works. This is no easy war; we must fight hard and with determination. Paul uses the word "wrestle" to describe how we must fight the enemy.

If you have ever seen a wrestling match, you know it isn't pretty. It's sweaty, sticky, dirty, and painful. When you wrestle, you get down and get dirty. There's no half-hearted involvement. You give it everything you've got, or you lose.

I know a bit about wrestling because my brother, Arthur, was the Maryland state wrestling champion in his weight class. At his championship match my brother weighed in at about 230 pounds and was going up against the three-time Maryland state champion who out-weighed him

Danville Public Library
Danville, Illinois

by 35 pounds. Before the match, a reporter asked, "Who is the toughest wrestler in this room?"

My brother, humble fellow that he is, said, "You're looking at him!"

The reporter looked at him and asked, "What makes you think you're so tough? You're about to fight the man who has won the state championship three times in a row."

My brother replied with a very insightful comment, "I know. He's bigger and perhaps stronger than I am, but I know his methods."

That match was a war. You heard thumps, grunts, and groans. You saw blood, pain, and anguish. But when it was over, my brother had won. He later explained, "I couldn't win by strength 'cause he was too strong. But I understood his moves and knew how to counter them."

My brother had studied his enemy's moves. He knew the tricks his opponent would try. So he learned how to defeat those moves. With that knowledge, he fought hard and won.

We are in a similar fight against Satan. Just as my brother needed to learn his opponent's moves, we need to understand Satan's moves. We need to know how he operates, so that we can prepare ourselves "to resist in the evil day, and having done everything, to stand firm" (Ephesians 6:13). No place in Scripture reveals Satan's schemes better than Genesis 3, which records Satan's initial contact with man. As the story unfolds, we clearly see Satan's strategy to ruin the human race.

## To Create Disunity

Satan's first strategy is to divide and conquer. He knows God doesn't work where there is confusion (1 Corinthians 14:33, 40), division, or disharmony. So the primary way Satan causes havoc in God's program is to create disunity, confusion, and disharmony in God's family. That is what he did with Adam and Eve, and the effects were disastrous.

When Adam and Eve ate the fruit God had forbidden, Satan succeeded in destroying the unity God intended for their marriage relationship, their family relationship, and their relationship with God (Genesis 3:7-19). He successfully put a stop to the good works God intended Adam and Eve to accomplish through their lives and family.

God not only demands unity in marriage and family relationships, but in His church as well. Our God is a God of unity. It is against His nature to work in the midst of division. That is why in His high priestly prayer (John 17) Jesus repeatedly prayed that "they may be one, just as We are one." Jesus knew that Satan would try to destroy the church through disunity. Thus, He earnestly prayed that the church would be a unified body through which God could accomplish His work.

God's insistence on unity is why so much of the New Testament gives instruction for maintaining the unity of the church. For example, 1 Corinthians 14:40 instructs the church to do all things properly and in order. Ephesians 4:3 exhorts believers to be "diligent to preserve the unity of the Spirit in the bond of peace." Peter tells husbands to live with their wives in an understanding way, otherwise God will not hear their prayers (1 Peter 3:7).

The same way the stability of the family has everything to do with the stability of the local community, the unity of the church has everything to do with the overall state of society. If, for example, families become dysfunctional, juvenile delinquency is likely to increase (which is exactly what happened when Cain killed his brother, Abel). When the church is in disarray, the spiritual glue of society is weakened, which opens the door for moral deterioration. Disunity, then, opens the door for Satan to promote his agenda in the world.

Satan recognizes the power of God's people. He knows that we are the only ones in the world who can keep him from messing up God's plan. So he is desperate to stop us. That is why the church is always under attack from Satan. He wants to get choir folks fighting each other. He wants to get church leaders fighting each other. He wants to get members fighting each other. He wants husbands and wives to be fighting each other. If he succeeds, God's people become ineffective.

As God's people, we must overcome disunity before we can fight any other battles. When we see disunity, we should not join Satan's side and keep it going. We should stop, recognize the source, and act under God's authority to restore our unity so He can continue His work through us.

## To Make Us Think that He Is God

Satan's second strategy is to get us to believe that he is God—or at least God's very close friend. Satan is a diabolical schemer who knows how to put on the right clothes. He makes himself look acceptable, even respectable. That is how he approached Eve.

The first thing he did was to talk about God (Genesis 3:1), and Eve talked right back. Naive Eve thought she was having a conversation about God when in fact she was talking to the devil about how to *rebel* against God.

Satan does the same thing today. He will get us to talk about God perpetually. He doesn't mind talking about God *as long as he can influence what we believe about God*. The New Testament says that Satan is a great counterfeiter. He covers himself up so that he looks innocent. And he is so easy to talk with. What he says sounds so good. He uses just enough nice God talk so we don't know he's about to "rip us off." Rather than approaching us dressed in a red jump suit with horns on his head and a pitchfork in his hand, he comes as an angel of light (2 Corinthians 2:14). That's why he's so successful in promoting his program through religion; he looks as much like God as possible.

Satan's network of assistants is formidable as well. He has counterfeit ministers who represent his interests and communicate to his children (2 Corinthians 11:15). He has counterfeit churches who house his institution (Revelation 2:9) and counterfeit Christians who execute his program (Matthew 25). This elaborate system works to destroy us and our society by getting us to operate under the authority of a false god, while simultaneously getting us to think that we believe in and serve the true God.

## To Make Us Forget the Consequences of Sin

When God put man in the Garden, He gave specific instructions: "From any tree of the garden you may eat freely; but from the tree of the knowledge of good and evil you shall not eat, for in the day that you eat from it you shall surely die" (Genesis 2:16-17).

The consequences of God's command were clear: "You shall surely die!" But when Eve answered Satan's inquiry about the tree, she minimized God's wrath. The words she used indicated some doubt about the result—the consequence *might* be death. That was all Satan needed to keep her moving toward rebellion against God.

Some of us test God in the same way. We think we *might* die, that we *might* get into trouble. However, we dare not misquote God. His words are clear. When He says "surely," He doesn't mean maybe, could be, or might be. He means, "Don't mess with Me! These are the consequences, and there will be no discussion about them!"

We must know what God's Word says, for if we don't, we open the door to Satan's influence and control. Some of us are too liberal. We say "might die" when God says "surely die." Others of us are too strict and add to God's rules. With Eve we say, "We must not eat or touch," when God only said, "Don't eat." We must stand where Scripture stands—not adding to it or subtracting from it.

No matter what Satan does to make us doubt the consequences of sin, we must not believe him. He entices us with what feels good, but he never tells us the whole story. He says, "See how good it looks"; but he never adds, "Of course, it will kill you." Even when we can't see them, sin has consequences. We always pay for sin. Sin is a bit like buying on credit. We can spend now and pay later—but pay we will, and the interest is a whopper.

## TO MAKE US FORGET GOD'S GOODNESS
## AND ACT INDEPENDENTLY OF HIM

Satan picked up on Eve's doubt about the consequences of sin and fueled her doubt about God. As soon as he saw her weakness, he worked to intensify it: "You surely shall not die. For God knows that in the day you eat from it your eyes will be opened, and you will be like God, knowing good and evil" (Genesis 3:4-5).

Eve already had an inappropriate view of God because she doubted the consequences of His Word. So Satan's next step was to get her to doubt His goodness. To do this, Satan gave Eve a lesson in theology—his own version. In effect he said, "Let me tell you something about God. He's holding out on you."

We don't know how many trees were in the garden. There may have been hundreds or thousands, and God said only one tree was forbidden. Of course, that's the one Satan wanted to talk about. Eve should have said, "Yes, I can't eat from that tree, but I can from that one and that one and that one and that one and . . ." But she didn't do that. She began to look only at that one tree. As she looked at it, she began to crave the one and only thing she couldn't have.

We're just like Eve. We can look at all of God's blessings and say, "But God, there's this one thing I really want. I don't know why I can't have it. If You really loved me, You'd give it to me." We must remember that God doesn't deny us something because He is stingy. God is good. He wants us to enjoy the fullness of His goodness. When He says, "No, you can't have that," it's because He wants to protect us—to keep us from dying.

I like to think of God's restrictions as similar to the sidelines in a football game. The sidelines enhance the game; they don't destroy it. Football wouldn't be much fun if play could extend into the stands and the concession area, and onto the parking lot. That would be chaos. Yet we have chaos in our society because we have rebelled against God's standards. As our unbridled passions, unrestricted greed, and rampant selfishness continue to dominate our lives, we can only expect to experience what Eve experienced—the trickery of Satan himself.

Just as the sidelines enable thousands of people to enjoy a football game because the contest is confined to appropriate boundaries, our obedience to God's moral boundaries can restore our nation to the full enjoyment of His blessings. The game of life can be played to its fullest only on God's morally restricted field of play.

Satan's next step was to get Eve to act on her own. He got her to act on her feelings rather than on fact. He made her feel that the fruit was so desirable that she couldn't live without it. He got her to believe that feeling good was so important that she ignored what God said. By playing on her emotions, Satan got Eve to act independently of God.

God wants our *total* loyalty and commitment. He wants every area of our lives—even every thought—to be under His influence. He claims the right to have first place in everything: "For by Him all things were created, both in the heavens and on earth, visible and invisible, whether thrones or dominions or rulers or authorities—all things have been created by Him and for Him . . . so that He Himself might come to have first place in everything" (Colossians 1:16-18).

Satan, too, although he has no rightful claim to us, wants to have first place. In a way, Satan's job isn't tough. To elevate himself to first place all he has to do is entice us to act independently of God. When this happens, we have placed something under our control; we have usurped God's right to first place, because whatever is under *our* control is not under *God's* control. When we are independent of God, we are dependent on Satan, who gladly responds to our dependency.

## To Make Us Miss Out on God's Will for Us

After Adam and Eve ate the fruit, Genesis 3:7 says that they knew they were naked and had to cover themselves. After eating the fruit, everything changed. They had been naked all along and were doing fine. But Satan provided them with information they didn't need to know, so they covered themselves. They suddenly began to miss out on what God had intended for their relationship. Satan wants us to miss out on the will of God too. He wants each of us to ignore God's Word so that we die without ever knowing why we were born.

Ultimately, the greatest tragedy of missing out on God's will was that Adam and Eve lost fellowship with God, which meant losing the benefits of the Garden. Genesis 3:24 says that God drove them out of the Garden—out of fellowship with Him. That may seem like a harsh penalty for eating a piece of fruit, but fruit wasn't the issue. The issue—the choice—was, "Which god will you serve?"

By eating the fruit that God had forbidden, Adam and Eve essentially said, "You are no longer our God. We no longer desire Your kingdom. Satan is our lord, his kingdom is our goal, and our desire is to serve him." God in essence responded by saying, "If that's the way you are going to live, then get out."

The loss of mankind's fellowship with God and participation in His will has staggering repercussions for individuals, families, and nations. Fellowship with God alone produces purpose in life. A lack of purpose in life eventually leads to despair that we try to alleviate with drugs, sex, and materialism. Purposelessness in families is evidenced by no-fault divorces, abuse of wives and children, incest, and a desire for perpetual entertainment.

Madison Avenue finds it easy to profit from our purposelessness. It can advertise us into oblivion—and into debt. As soon as we have bought into the latest and greatest gimmick, it is made "new and improved." So we never experience relief from our purposelessness.

Our culture at large is also experiencing a traumatic loss of meaning. We see leaders on the take, abortion on demand, and murder for thrills. We pay psychiatrists $200 an hour to help us make sense of our moral madness. We buy guns to secure our safety. We elect politicians to lead us out of this maze. While we're busy doing these things, we miss the one and only thing that can solve our dilemma: returning to the Judeo-Christian ethic that is founded on biblical morality. Just as Satan failed to inform Eve that her rebellion would result in the loss of her family, her marital harmony, the life of one of her sons, her peace and tranquility, and ultimately her own life, we too have been duped into believing that we can live in rebellion against God and still have a meaningful culture.

## GOD CAN DEFEAT ALL SATAN'S STRATEGIES

We are fighting against a master schemer. He has been around longer than all of humanity put together. He has fought in every battle possible. He can pull out scheme after scheme after scheme to get us to act on our own and ignore God. He can and will do *anything* to destroy God's people and the human race. So there's no point to taking on the devil ourselves. He is too strong.

But there is good news. Satan is already a defeated enemy. He was defeated by God at Calvary. Although Satan has opened the gates of hell against God's people who seek to accomplish His work, God has given us the keys to open the doors of heaven to defeat any problem Satan sends our way.

Jesus told His disciples about those keys: ". . . upon this rock I will build My church; and the gates of Hades shall not overpower it. I will give you the keys of the kingdom of heaven; and whatever you shall bind on earth shall be bound in heaven, and whatever you shall loose on earth shall be loosed in heaven" (Matthew 16:18-19). Of course, we're in big trouble if we don't know where our keys are. We're in big trouble if we don't know how to use those keys. We're also in big trouble if we try to use the keys to unlock anything other than the doors of heaven. Heaven's keys only work in heaven's doors, and only heaven's doors can unleash heaven's power to overcome hell's onslaught.

Be assured, however, that we have access to heaven's keys. Revelation 1:12-13 tells us that the keys we need to open heaven's doors against the gates of hell are recorded in the Word of God. Even Jesus used God's Word against Satan. When Satan tempted Him, Jesus' consistent reply began, "It is written . . ." Jesus knew that resisting the devil requires more than closing our eyes and saying, "I resist. I resist. I resist." Resisting the devil means to positively use God's Word in the unity of the Body to accomplish God's will. Satan is frightened of Scripture because he is powerless before God's Word. When God's people wield Scripture in spiritual battles, Satan starts running.

Our world is in a tragic state. Many visible social problems cry out for healing. However, only spiritual people with spiritual power can fight spiritual battles. As God's people, the church has the means to fight the visible problems of our world. But we must fight them with spiritual solutions. As Paul says in 2 Corinthians 10:3, "For though we walk in the flesh, we do not war according to the flesh." Unless God's people recognize the true nature of the battle and fight right, they will never make an impact on society. Unless the church applies the Bible's truths to every aspect of life, there is no hope for society.

# 4

# The Failure of the Church

I f we look at the religious activity in our country today, it would appear
that we are in a Christian renaissance. We can attend churches, each
with its pastor and staff, in virtually every city and town. We can tune into
many Christian radio and television broadcasts. We can shop in thousands
of Christian bookstores and purchase books and study materials on any spiritual topic. We can study at scores of Christian colleges and universities.
We can work for hundreds of different Christian ministries. The visibility
of Christianity in the marketplace continues to grow.

Yet, if we look at our society at large, it appears to be increasingly
decadent. There are more marriage seminars and more divorces, more psychiatrists and more suicides, more financial counseling and more debt, more
"just say no" programs and more teenage pregnancies and drug abuse, more
community organizations and less transformation. There are more youth
groups yet more gangs, more income yet less giving, more sermons yet less
ministry.

How can these realities occur simultaneously? How can such a proliferation of Christian activity have so little impact on society? One expla-
nation can account for the coexistence of these contradictory realities: in
spite of all the Bible translations, all the study materials, and all the Bible
teachers, the church—God's people—fails to be what God has called it to
be.

Now, when I speak of the failure of the church, I am speaking of the
people of God as a collective group. There are certainly many, many indi-

vidual Christians, dynamic local churches led by godly pastors, and parachurch organizations that are having a solid biblical impact on the people and communities they serve. However, when you talk about turning around a whole culture gone astray, it will take a lot more than individual Christians and ministries having an impact. There will have to be a corporate impact of God's people on the total fabric of society.

## WE HAVE NOT ALLOWED JESUS TO BUILD HIS CHURCH

In Matthew 16:18, Jesus says, "I will build My church." On the surface it appears that He has indeed built quite a church. According to the American Church List (1989), we have 330,000 Protestant churches in our nation, with a total membership of 112 million people. The Gallup organization reports that 50 million Americans claim to be "born again."

However, Jesus' statement did not end with the words "I will build My church." He also said, "And the gates of Hades shall not overpower it." This qualifying statement forces us to look a little closer at how the church functions in the world.

If we understand that God intends His church to be a powerful force in society—a force powerful enough to lessen the effects of sin, then we have to admit that hell seems to be doing a good job of stopping the church. The church today is not the powerful, redeeming influence on society that it is supposed to be. Yet, if Jesus said that hell cannot stop His church, then it is surely impossible for hell to stop it. So if the church as we know it is being stopped, then what we see must not be His church.

The fundamental problem that we—God's people—face today is that we have not allowed Jesus to build *His* church. We have not dedicated ourselves to understanding and obeying God's instructions for the church. Instead, we have done things our way; we have built *our* church and put His name on top. And that's not good enough.

A church built by man's agenda rather than God's is satisfied with altar calls but lacks the discipline to make disciples. It's a place where homosexuals can sing in the choir. It's a place where adulterers can serve as leaders, yet have no accountability to the church nor receive discipline from the church. It's a place where preachers tell nice little anecdotes but do very little exposition of God's Word. It's a place where people are not exposed to Scripture or held accountable to obey it. Such is not what God wants His church to be.

God is greatly displeased when we build our *own* churches instead of building *His* church. We see this in Revelation 2 and 3, where John reveals Jesus' message to the seven churches of Asia. Jesus expressed His pleasure with the church but also conveyed a stern warning about its failures. He demanded that each church clean itself up, or He would do the cleaning—and His cleaning would carry dire consequences.

One of the ways God disciplines the local church (Revelation 2:5) is to remove the lampstand—His spiritual empowerment—from the church. I believe that's what is happening today. We see a lot of church activity—a lot of smoke—but little impact. The church has focused on its own agenda rather than on Christ's agenda. Thus, the light of the church has gone out. As a result, our world is deteriorating but not because sinners are sinning. After all, what else are they supposed to do? The tragedy is that the church has failed to be God's church. Therefore, the group God works through to salvage the culture cannot be found.

Jesus said that we alone are the light of the world (Matthew 5:14). The world is in darkness; it doesn't know how to deal with the weight of sin and its accompanying social problems. The world doesn't understand that all problems ultimately have a spiritual cause and, therefore, can only be solved by spiritual people with spiritual solutions. If the world is to see how to deal with the problems, it must follow the light of the church. The problem is, our lights aren't shining. Even worse, the church often looks to the darkness of the world and expects *it* to shine.

As God's people go, so goes the culture. Until we decide to be His church rather than a group of religious-looking people, our society is hopeless. Until we return to a spiritual frame of reference—recognizing the spiritual reality that is behind the physical reality—we cannot be light. Until we decide to become alternatives for God, bringing the light of divine options to our culture, there is no hope.

## WE HAVE FORGOTTEN WHAT WE ARE SUPPOSED TO BE

For the most part, the church today has forgotten its purpose. The church has mistakenly defined itself in terms of a building where people gather once a week so they feel good enough to make it through the next week. That's not the purpose of the church; it's merely a benefit. The sole purpose of the church is to be the dynamic, living body through which God can accomplish His work to His glory.

The church has not identified itself as a collection of believers who understand that their role as a community is to infiltrate the culture with God's righteousness. Thus, there is an absence of biblical Christianity lived out in society. The church includes people who are saved and are individually righteous, but the church lacks an understanding of the role of corporate righteousness in society.

At one time, the presence of biblical righteousness was evident in our culture. A generation or two ago, the church influenced the climate of our society. That didn't mean that everyone was a Christian. It didn't mean that the church ruled over society like a harsh taskmaster. However, society did benefit from the positive effects of the righteousness of God's people. The church had an impact on how people behaved toward one another.

For example, I grew up in an inner-city neighborhood in Baltimore. If I happened to do something wrong and an adult saw me, I was in trouble. It didn't matter if I was ten blocks away from home. It didn't matter if the adult didn't even know me. If I did something I wasn't supposed to do, it was perfectly all right for the adult who saw me to grab me by the collar, spank me, and say, "Boy, you know your mother wouldn't want you to do that!"

Then the adult who caught me would walk me to my house, knock on the door, and tell my mother what I'd done. My mother would look at the person kindly and say, "Thank you for caring enough to discipline my son. Won't you please come in and have some tea?"

My mother and her newfound friend would enjoy their tea and cookies and talk about why kids seem to get into so much trouble. After a while, my mother's new friend would leave. After my mother said goodbye, she'd spank me again because someone else had had to correct me.

When I was growing up, there was a moral code in society. People understood how they were to behave toward each another and held one another accountable. That moral code was rooted in the righteousness of God's people.

That moral code no longer exists. The church has turned aside from God's agenda and set the world free to do what it naturally does when it is estranged from God—sin. The world is doing just what it's supposed to do; the result is lawlessness.

Unfortunately, the church seems to have little insight into how to fix the problem it has unleashed. We have forgotten that we alone, as God's people, are His agents for making a spiritual impact on the culture. God placed His church on earth so that hell can see what heaven looks like when heaven resides in its midst. Therefore, we are to model Christ in every aspect of life and thereby preserve the culture from the destruction of sin.

Our world is in great trouble because it doesn't know how to fix Mr. Dumpty. However, the greater tragedy is that the *church* has forgotten how to fix Mr. Dumpty. In fact, much of the church has even forgotten that it is *supposed* to know how to fix Mr. Dumpty.

### WE HAVE FORGOTTEN WHO CREATED OUR AGENDA

Secular organizations regularly ask the church to bless and participate in their agenda. These organizations want to link up with the church because the church has access to people. They want to accomplish their goals through the church. But that's not how the church is supposed to work. We have forgotten that there is no division between the sacred and the secular. We have forgotten that we can't rightly understand what happens on earth unless we start with "In the beginning, God." We have forgotten that our agenda starts and stops with God.

This fact is dramatically portrayed in Joshua 5:13-14. In this account, Joshua was preparing for battle when he saw a great man standing before him. The man was dressed in battle array, with his sword drawn, ready to fight—an intimidating character. Joshua was concerned about this great warrior, so he asked the man whose side he was on. If this mighty captain was on Israel's side, Joshua could be assured of success. However, if he was on the enemy's side, Joshua knew Israel was in trouble. The mighty warrior gave Joshua an unexpected answer. He explained that he was captain of the Lord's army. As captain of the Lord's army, he hadn't come to take sides; he had come to take over.

The church has failed to understand this truth today. God isn't about to join anyone's side. He has come to take over. He is doing only one thing—*His* thing. He has come to carry out His program according to *His* methods. The church does not follow the world order. The church is not the means by which the world accomplishes its goals. The church is the means by which God—and God alone—accomplishes His goals. Therefore, the church sets the agenda, not the world. If the world wants solutions, it ought to follow us; we ought not to follow it.

That's not the way the church is working today. Rather than the world coming to the church for solutions, the church begs the world for solutions. For example, the church has often surrendered its rightful agenda to political programs. It has hopped on the backs of donkeys and elephants, hoping they will provide solutions to society's problems. The black church often depends on the Democratic Party and its quest for social justice. The white church often depends on the Republican Party in its quest for morality. Neither church fully realizes that no political party fully functions according to God's agenda. Therefore, neither party can rightfully demand the church's allegiance.

Likewise, secular organizations that deal with social problems often set the agenda for the church. Although many of them have made tremendous contributions to society, they often do not use divine means to accomplish divine ends. When the church joins forces with these organizations, who sets the agenda? All too often it is not God, not the church. The church simply jumps aboard and rides the existing agenda, which tends to be political and social rather than theological and spiritual.

The church must remember where the battle lies. We fight "not against flesh and blood" (Ephesians 6:12). The fight is a spiritual fight that can only be fought by spiritual people. When the church follows an agenda that is set by people who are not spiritual, it is not following the right agenda.

We have to be aware of where our agenda comes from, even within the church. God's people often gather to pray about what the church does. We ask God to bless this activity and that program. But we often fail to find out if the programs and activities we plan are what God wants us to do. Then we wonder why God doesn't seem to answer our prayers.

There's a reason for His apparent silence. God doesn't exist to bless our agenda. He will only bless His agenda as it is carried out His way (Matthew 6:10). When we start to pray about how to pull off His agenda in His way, then we're praying about something He is a part of. Then we'll start to see His blessing (Numbers 14:11-20).

However, most of us have forgotten that God sets the agenda and that God's agenda is our only legal agenda. Most of us have forgotten that we have been "predestined according to the plan of him who works out everything in conformity with the purpose of his will" (Ephesians 1:11). Most of us have forgotten that we are to set the agenda for the world to follow.

The results are tragic. Instead of setting the agenda for society, the church has been crippled by society. Instead of leading the parade, the church is not even marching in it. Instead of presenting a divine alternative in society, the church is being run by society. The church is no longer the church in the world; rather, the world is in the church.

## WE HAVE JOINED FORCES WITH THE WORLD

During the first century after Christ lived on earth, His disciples were closely aligned with God's agenda. They knew their purpose, and they turned the world upside down. Today it's more accurate to say that the world turns the church upside down.

In the human body, the immune system prevents disease from destroying the body. But in the disease we call AIDS, the immune system stops functioning properly. It is unable to successfully fight off the germs and viruses that attack the body. Because of this failure the common cold can easily become a fatal case of pneumonia.

Society, too, has an immune system that protects it from the destruction of sin. That immune system is the church. However, the church suffers from the disease of spiritual AIDS, which has greatly diminished its effectiveness. The church is having so much intercourse with the world that it has become sick. With such an affliction, the church has lost its spiritual strength; it has lost its ability to ward off the evil forces that would conquer it and has also lost its ability to protect society from the devastating consequences of the viruses and bacteria of sin.

Like the world, the church has failed to recognize the authority of Scripture. We conveniently accept what we wish to and reject that which we view as old-fashioned or irrelevant. We have taken what God calls sin and given it a more palatable identity. Rather than functioning as a peculiar people committed to God's agenda, the church functions as warmed-over, humanistic religion. It's not so much that God's people have stopped believing in God but that they have chosen to believe in a humanistic God—a God who gives out ten *suggestions*, not Ten *Commandments*.

We have allowed ourselves to become so mixed up with the world's agenda, standards, and methodologies that we have lost our identity as God's people. By spinelessly adopting the world's standards, the church has failed to judge itself according to God's standards. It has failed to make itself pure for God's use.

Because the church can't get its own house in order, it has very little to say to the broader society. Plagued with moral and financial scandals and rebellious and ungodly leaders, the church's pale effectiveness is overlooked by the world. The fact that political leaders and congressmen ignore prophetic utterances from the church is no accident. It's a direct result of the church's failure to commit itself to God's agenda.

Like the world, we have anesthetized ourselves with VCRs, movies, sports events, and television programs, and we have looked for the easy solutions. We have allowed the state to become the primary educator of our children. We have used secular television as a convenient baby-sitter. We have allowed secular courts to judge church disputes.

Instead of diligently pursuing what God would have us do, we look for what seems to work in secular society, add a Bible verse, and say we have biblically based programs. In reality, such programs are nothing more than warmed-over secularism. God will not be compromised. He will not participate in the world's agenda, no matter how noble the goal may be.

Since we have put the world's agenda ahead of God's, we have lost the ability to bring God's long-term, spiritually oriented solutions to society's problems. We have become dependent upon the world for solutions. The church actually spends much more time seeking direction from the world than the world spends seeking guidance from the church.

That isn't the way it is supposed to be. The world should be coming to us. The world should be looking at us and asking, "How do you get your stuff to work?" It is time for the church to be God's alternative in the world. It is time for the church to provide God's perspective and God's solutions to Mr. Dumpty's problems. It is time for the church to seek, obey, and fulfill its mission in the world.

# 5

## Hope for a Sick Society

"These men turn the world upside down." That was how secular society described the Christian church of the first century (Acts 17:6). Their statement was an acknowledgment that the presence of Christians transformed the social order. Wherever Paul went to proclaim the gospel and establish a fellowship of believers, cultural impact occurred. In Thessalonica, for instance, riots broke out (Acts 17:1-9). In Corinth, Christian influence was so strong that political means were sought to halt its spread (Acts 18:1-17). In Ephesus, the gospel's impact on people's lives shook up the economic order (Acts 19:20-41).

God never intended the social impact of the church to be limited to the first century; He intended social impact to be normative for the church at all times. When the church is being the church as God intended it, it has to make a difference in society because God's program is not neutral. Consider for a moment the impact Jesus has on people: we can hate Him and seek His destruction, or we can love Him and submit to His lordship. But we can't ignore Him. His presence calls for a response.

Likewise, society's response to the church ought not to be neutral. Since we speak for God, our words and deeds should clearly proclaim that God's agenda is not subject to the world's political and social structures. God's agenda stands above everything on earth. Therefore, the world should either join with God's people or reject them, but it should not be able to ignore them.

## GOD'S PEOPLE CAN IMPACT SOCIETY

As God's people, we have the ability to make an impact on society. We can, *and we must.* Christ came to earth to destroy the works of the devil (1 John 3:8). When we operate under His authority, we are the only entity on earth that can defeat the works of the devil. But to be effective in the battle, we must know who we are and how we are to live. We must realize that we exist for a spiritual purpose. We have a divinely mandated mission to accomplish.

We read about two wealthy men in Genesis 13: Abraham and his nephew, Lot. One man knew his spiritual purpose and pursued it; the other failed to understand his spiritual role in society.

These men, their families, and their business enterprises occupied the same territory. However, the land wasn't sufficient to sustain all their needs. In time, their hired hands began scrapping about available resources. So Abraham approached Lot and in essence said, "Things are getting a bit tense around here, Lot. We've got to keep peace in the family, and the only way I see to do that is to split up the territory and go our separate ways. You can have first choice. Whatever way you choose, I'll go the other."

Lot considered his options and chose the beautiful, well-watered Jordan valley, where the cities of Sodom and Gomorrah were located. From a business point of view, he couldn't have made a better choice. But Lot's decision lacked spiritual insight because Genesis 13:13 says, "Now the men of Sodom were wicked exceedingly and sinners against the Lord."

Lot moved into a nasty environment—one full of lust, oppression, and corruption. His world was much like ours. Sin of every variety was practiced to its fullest. Sodom was full of great ministry opportunities.

Lot, however, wasn't big on ministry. He was more concerned about affluence and personal peace. The Bible tells us that Lot was a righteous man; the sin in Sodom wrenched his soul (2 Peter 2:7-8). But Lot didn't want to upset anybody, so he kept quiet about the sin around him. He forgot that his main purpose was to spread God's kingdom, so his faith wasn't active in society. He had a great private religion, but he didn't have corporate impact. And corporate impact was desperately needed.

One day, while God and Abraham were having a theological discussion, God announced that things were so bad in Sodom and Gomorrah that He was going to wipe the cities off the map (Genesis 18:20-21; 19:13). Abraham was taken aback by God's proposal. He understood why God would want to wipe the horrible sin of those cities off the map. But he could not understand why God—the deliverer of His people—would also destroy the righteous people who lived there.

So Abraham—not without some fear—made a counter-proposal to God: "Suppose there are fifty righteous within the city; wilt Thou indeed sweep it away and not spare the place for the sake of the fifty righteous who are in it? Far be it from Thee to do such a thing" (Genesis 18:24-25a). Abraham was banking on the premise that the presence of God's people would save the cities.

He was right. God agreed that if there were fifty righteous people in the cities He would spare the multitude of unrighteous people (Genesis 18:26). God was willing to spare the cities not because the sinners deserved it, but because His people were still representing Him there even in the midst of horrible sin. As long as God's people were doing their job—bringing God's presence to bear on all aspects of life—there was hope that things would change for the better.

After striking his deal with God, Abraham had a new problem. He couldn't find fifty righteous people. Things were so bad that he had to whittle God down to accepting only ten righteous people in all of Sodom and Gomorrah. We know he had one righteous man, Lot. Lot had a wife, two daughters, and two sons-in-law. That makes six. If Lot had won his family over to God and each of them had won just one other person, there would have been twelve righteous people—more than enough to spare the cities.

But Lot's righteousness was so private he hadn't even made an impact on his family, much less on the society that surrounded him. When Lot told his sons-in-law that they needed to leave because God was about to destroy the city, they laughed. They thought it was a big joke. Only his wife and daughters left with him. While they were running away, Lot's wife thought about some of the nice things she was leaving behind. So she turned back—just for a longing look—and became a pillar of salt. Later, Lot's daughters got him drunk so they could have children by him, showing that they were more influenced by the corrupt culture they had left behind than by God's righteousness as demonstrated in their father's life. Lot failed to be the man God needed him to be in Sodom. The consequences of his failure are sobering indeed.

The lessons to be learned from Lot's story apply directly to Christians today. Sin in our society—as in Sodom—is out of control. Our society is approaching destruction. Like Lot, many Christians today are playing Christianity. Apart from Sundays, most of us show little evidence that we belong to the kingdom. Our righteousness is personal and private. It is a righteousness that says, "I truly believe that this or that is wrong, but I won't speak out or tell anyone else how to live." So we piously close our eyes to the evil that surrounds us. We're not serious about impacting culture. For the most part, we're only serious about our personal peace and affluence. That is not what God has called His people to be.

## GOD'S PEOPLE ARE THE ONLY HOPE

In His Sermon on the Mount, Jesus made clear what the church is to be and how it is to impact the world. He explained that His disciples were the only ones who could bring His perspective to society. So He explained what kingdom people are supposed to be like, how they are to function, and how they are different from nonkingdom people. He said, "You are the salt of the earth. . . . You are the light of the world. . . . Let your light shine before men in such a way that they may see your good works, and glorify your Father who is in heaven" (Matthew 5:13-16). These two metaphors—salt and light—illustrate the role of God's people in the world.

The first point is that Jesus isn't talking about the relationship of salt to salt or light to light. He speaks about the relationship of salt to the earth and light to the world. So if we are concerned about the earth, we'd better know something about salt; if we are concerned about the world, we'd better know something about light. The only way the earth will get the help it needs is if it has salt; the only way the world will get the help it needs is if the light is shining.

The second crucial point of this passage isn't very clear in our English Bibles. However, in the Greek text, the position of the word "you" indicates that Jesus meant that "you and you alone" are the salt of the earth. His church is the only entity that can ever be salt to the earth. Nothing else—not charities, politics, or causes—can ever become salt. Only God's people are salt.

Yet many of God's people today either never knew or have forgotten that they alone are the salt of the earth. As a result, they have jumped on the world's solutions and are amazed when those solutions don't sprinkle salt on the earth's misery. Only God's people can be salt. And if God's people are not salt, then the earth is in trouble; it has no hope. Like Sodom and Gomorrah, a saltless earth will be destroyed.

## GOD'S PEOPLE ARE THE SALT OF THE WORLD

*Salt preserves that which would otherwise decay.* For thousands of years, particularly before the widespread use of refrigeration, people salted meat to preserve it. Salt is an antibacterial agent that prevents decay. In the absence of salt, bacteria causes meat to go bad. One thing God wants His people to do is to preserve the earth by rendering His divine judgment on it. The earth is covered with a bacteria called sin, and we are the salt that can protect it. Our job as salt is to be on the meat—not to be having a happy time in the saltshaker. If the salt isn't out where the bacteria is, the salt doesn't do any good. What ought to excite us about being God's people is not that we have a great church service on Sunday but that, when we go out into the earth on Monday, the meat is doing better. Often that isn't the case. We have so much fun in the saltshaker that we allow the meat to decay.

*Salt also stimulates growth and production.* In Jesus' day, farmers mixed salt with the soil to enhance the yield. In a similar way, Christians under the control of the Holy Spirit ought to produce an abundance of righteousness in society. If our lives are not producing anything, then we're not being the kind of salt God created us to be.

Finally, *salt produces thirst.* Salt's ability to produce thirst is the reason bars and night clubs provide free, salt-laden snacks such as peanuts and pretzels for their customers. These are not provided because of the owners' love for their patrons but because of the thirst-producing power of the salt. As soon as the snack dishes are depleted, they are replenished. There is always plenty of salt to keep the drink orders coming.

In a similar way, the church should be producing thirst in society. The impact of our ministry should be creating thirst in all who come into contact with us. After they encounter God's people, the people of this world ought to be spiritually thirsty. They ought to be thirsty enough that they start looking for something to quench their thirst. They ought to be able to look at us and see that Jesus Christ, the living water, is the only one who satisfies (John 4:13-14).

Salt is an important commodity. We cannot survive without it. Yet after Jesus said, "You are the salt of the earth," He added a qualification: "but if the salt has become tasteless, how will it be made salty again? It is good for nothing anymore, except to be thrown out and trampled under foot by men" (Matthew 5:13).

How can salt possibly lose its saltiness? The reason salt is salty is because it is salt. It can't be anything other than salt. However, when salt is mixed up with another substance, it changes. The other substance doesn't become salty, but the potency of the salt is diminished to the point that it may not even be seen or tasted.

For example, in the Middle East salt and gypsum are mixed together to make a thick paste that is used to waterproof the flat roofs of houses. This salt and gypsum paste not only seals out water, it makes a solid base that can be walked on. In the Middle East, roofs of houses are social gathering places. Kids don't have backyards to play in, so they play on rooftops.

People don't have porches, so they have parties and wedding receptions on rooftops.

Jesus knew exactly what He was talking about. When salt loses its potency by being mixed up with gypsum, it is worthless as salt. It is only good for being trampled underfoot. Likewise, if the church—the salt of the earth—mixes itself up with anything other than salt, its potency will be greatly diminished. The salt won't even be discernible in the new substance. When the church is mixed up with the world, it loses its distinctiveness, power, uniqueness, and potency. The church may still have its salty songs, salty-sounding preachers, and salty worship services, but when the world tastes it, the salt has lost its flavor.

If it is to make an impact on the world, the church must not mix itself up with the world. That's why Romans 12:2 says, "Do not be conformed to this world." We need to realize that conformity to the world doesn't mean going out and being the worst sinners on earth. All God's people need to do to be conformed to the world is to live like the world—independently of God's authority. When the church acts independently of God's authority, it becomes just another nice social program.

Salt doesn't have to be mixed with anything to be salt. It can do the job by itself. But the church has failed to understand that we and we alone can do the job, so we have conformed ourselves to the world. We have tried to see things and do things the way the world does rather than seeing and doing the way God does. As a result, we're not better salt; we don't even look, feel, or taste like salt. So the world walks right over us like we're not even there.

## GOD'S PEOPLE ARE THE LIGHT OF THE WORLD

In Matthew 5:14, Jesus told His gathered disciples that they were the light of the world. At that time, the world was the Roman Empire—a political union of millions of people. Jesus could make that statement because He knew that only a handful of men could change the whole world.

Light is so distinct from darkness that it only takes a small spot of light to make the darkness fly away. For example, all we need to control darkness is a flashlight; wherever we point that light, it overrules the darkness. The greater the darkness, the brighter the light will shine. It isn't necessary to have a great multitude of people to light up a spiritually dark world. Just a few bright lights can do the job.

Notice that Jesus didn't say, "Go out and get the light so you can brighten things up." He said, "You *are* the light." When you *are* something, you don't have to go find it. All you have to do is discover what you are.

There's a story about a little eagle that fell out of its nest and landed in a turkey farm. The eagle grew up among the turkeys and, although he looked a bit different, learned to waddle like a turkey, bob his head like a turkey, and act like a turkey.

One day the young eagle looked up into the sky and saw a beautiful eagle soaring above. The little eagle in the turkey yard thought, *Oh, I'd love to be able to do that!* As the eagle soared overhead, it looked down and saw the young eagle below. Suddenly it swooped down to the ground and asked, "What are you doing here?"

The little eagle replied, "I'm just here in the turkey yard where I've always been."

The great eagle looked and said, "Spread your wings, boy. You do just what I do. Follow me." Then he flapped his wings and lifted off the ground.

The young eagle tried it, too. "Wheee! This is all right!"

"See," the mature eagle said, "you've been living among these turkeys so long that you were beginning to believe you're something you're not! Follow me, and you'll find out what you really are."

"But I'm scared," the little eagle replied. "I won't know what to do when I get out of the turkey yard."

"When you get out of here, you'll find out," the big eagle answered.

So the little eagle began to soar and fly. He loved it. But the turkeys down below called out to him and said, "Hey little guy, what are you doing up there? You belong down here."

"No, I don't," called out the young eagle. "I used to belong there, but now I'm what I was created to be. I don't belong with you anymore."

Have you ever looked at a strong Christian and thought, *I wish I could be like that, I wish I could lead a ministry like that?* The reason you feel that way is because you are salt and light. What you see in that strong Christian is what God has created you to be. So you don't have to go around looking for the light you're supposed to be. You just have to be what you were created to be.

One of the things light does is show things as they really are. The world has a hard time seeing reality; it doesn't know what reality is anymore. In fact, because the world is in darkness it isn't supposed to be able see things as they are. However, the church is a different matter. Our eyes have been opened to the spiritual reality behind the physical. Thus, we are the light. We are supposed to be switching on the light in the darkness so that others can see. But instead I'm afraid we're joining the world in the darkness. Instead of transforming the world by light, we are being kept in darkness by the world.

That's not how light is supposed to work. When the sun rises in the morning, it takes over. It comes up and banishes every trace of darkness. That's what the church is supposed to do in the world—take over the darkness with light. Christianity is not passive. It ought to take over.

Thus, there's no room for "secret agent" Christians. The world ought to know who we are, why we are, and what we are doing. Jesus further explained this by saying,

> You are the light of the world. A city set on a hill cannot be hidden. Nor do men light a lamp, and put it under the peck measure, but on the lamp stand; and it gives light to all who are in the house. Let your light shine before men in such a way that they may see your good works, and glorify your Father who is in heaven. (Matthew 5:14-16)

In Jesus' day, cities were built of white limestone. If the city was on a hill, even the single flame of a candle would brighten the whiteness of the buildings, creating a beacon for nighttime travelers to follow. In a similar way, Jesus said that His people are on public display, serving as beacons of light so that the world will know what we are all about. Our light should not be hidden but should light everything within our sphere of influence. Everyone ought to know where we stand on abortion, on morality, on homelessness, on pornography.

Furthermore, Jesus tells us how our light ought to shine. He tells us what kind of bulbs to put into the lamp. We're not to let our light shine the way *we* want it to shine. Our light is to shine so that others will see our good works and glorify our heavenly Father.

## GOD'S PEOPLE ARE TO MINISTER IN THE WORLD

True ministry is getting out where the action is and touching lives. It is reaching out to the fatherless, the widows, the AIDS victims, the prisoners. Much of the so-called ministry of churches today is confined to the four walls of the church building. So our light never goes beyond those four walls.

Don't get me wrong. Being in church is good and necessary, but the world doesn't see our light when we're in church. I think of church as being similar to the huddle in a football game. A team gets in a huddle to figure out what the next play will be and to make sure everybody knows what to do to make it happen. But the 65,000 people sitting in the stadium didn't pay $25 to watch eleven guys huddle. They want to see what difference the huddle makes in the game. I'm afraid that many Christians today get high on the huddle. And while we're happy in the huddle, Satan is out there scoring touchdowns.

God's people are not doing God's good works when they're huddled up in the church. Our good works start when what happens on Sunday morning is transferred into the community on Monday. Our ministry is to be out in the world where our works can be seen—like the light of a city on a hill.

Furthermore, while we're doing good works in public, we must do them in such a way that they bring glory to God. We don't do good works for our own glory or because it's the right thing to do. We do good works for God's glory. We don't just feed the hungry so they will be fed; we feed them so that God will be seen. We don't get people off drugs just so they aren't addicted; we get them off drugs so they will see our Father. We don't stop abortions just so babies will live; we stop abortions so people will see God's hand in the life of every human being. We do all things to glorify God. When people see our works, they should "ooh and aah" at what God has done. The church is not just another charitable, social-service agency. Only the church can do good in a way that glorifies God.

# Part 2
# The Principles

# 6

# A Proper Definition of the Church

God has given the church the monumental task of infiltrating culture and bringing spiritual reality to bear on society's problems. He has given the church the responsibility and ability to put Mr. Dumpty together again. However, today's church has failed to accomplish the task to a significant degree. In fact, the great tragedy of our day is not that Mr. Dumpty lies shattered on the ground. The great tragedy is not that sinners are sinning. The great tragedy is that God's people—the saints who are not supposed to live like sinners—are often more sinful than the sinners.

One key reason God's people are unable to live as we ought is that many of us have been misled by an improper definition of the church. If the church is ever to become the powerful, redeeming force that God intends it to be, we must first understand what the church is supposed to be.

## ANALYZING OUR DEFINITION OF THE CHURCH

Many of God's people view the church as nothing more than a building where we go to pay spiritual homage every week. It's a place we go to see what we can get. We want an emotionally uplifting choir. We want the preacher to give us an inspirational sermon. We want a convenient parking spot. We want the ushers to give us a nice, clean place to sit. We want to hold a pretty bulletin that tells us what's happening. And when "church" is over, we want to be able to say, "Oh, I feel good this morning!

57

Preacher, you really blessed me today!"

All of this is nice, but it's only part of the story. If our definition of the church stops here, then we have a wrong definition. The church is much more than an ecclesiastical gathering. The church is to be an entity that touches every aspect of life and teaches God's people how to live. The church is the corporate community of God's people who represent and reflect the person and program of God in history.

The *church gathered* is where we meet with the corporate community of God's people to renew a divine frame of reference that guides our lives for the rest of the week. Church is where we receive a word from God. It is our preamble to the rest of the week. It is a dynamic gathering where God talks to His people and we talk to God. Church is where we submit to God as Lord of every part of life. The *church scattered* is when God's people, who have been renewed and refocused on Sunday, carry God's truth into society on Monday.

The church needs to rediscover what it means to be the church. We need to rediscover what it means for God's people to live all of life through a biblical frame of reference. We must rediscover how the church can be a dynamic, accountable entity that takes seriously its responsibility to reflect God's image in society. We must once again understand the nature and function of the church *as God intends it to be*. The starting point for this process of rediscovery is to realize anew who Jesus is.

### DISCOVERING WHO JESUS IS
### IN RELATION TO THE CHURCH

Toward the end of His ministry on earth, Jesus had a heart-to-heart talk with His disciples about His identity. He wanted to know what His disciples thought of what other people said about Him and what they personally understood about Him (Matthew 16:13-15). Jesus wanted to know if there was any qualitative difference between what the world thought about Him and what His disciples—those who had walked with Him—thought about Him.

Peter, always the first to speak, jumped right in and answered for the group: "Thou art the Christ, the Son of the living God" (v. 16). Peter often said the wrong thing, but this time he hit the bull's-eye. In effect, Peter said, "Jesus, we've all talked about this. We had to decide a while back if giving up our fishing and families to follow You was worth it. We concluded that yes, You are the Messiah. You are the Son of God—the one we've been waiting for!" What a powerful statement about the person and work of Jesus. Jesus is the one sent to redeem us—the divine Son of God.

What is the significance of realizing Jesus' identity? Once we recognize and agree upon who Jesus is, we have started the church. When we agree on who Jesus is and choose to follow Him, we begin to live and function as His people—the church. We begin to pursue the future in a new direction under His authority and through His power.

Unfortunately, some of us live as though salvation means we're finished, as though we have nothing left to do. But that's not the case. Salvation is just the beginning. When we get our passport to heaven, life isn't over; it's just begun. If we are saved, it is because Jesus found us. He singled us out—through no merit of our own—paid the price, revealed Himself to us, and called us to follow Him.

Jesus fully recognized the significance of the disciples' commitment to His identity. Because of their reply, He knew He had a group of people who could make an impact on society. So He continued the discussion by saying, "And I also say to you that you are Peter, and upon this rock I will build My church; and the gates of Hades shall not overpower it" (Matthew 16:18).

Library shelves are filled with explanations of this verse. However, I submit that it summarizes our entire reason for living. Once we recognize who Jesus is and submit to His lordship, our purpose for living is to be a part of His church in order to accomplish His work on earth. I believe Jesus singled Peter out as the spokesman for the group but made clear that His church couldn't be built on just one spokesman. Jesus was saying that He needed many people united together to build His church. Jesus envisioned His church as a massive slab, made up of many interconnected stones that would stand firm against the forces of hell.

As God's people, we are the stones Jesus is talking about. Together, we make up His church. As a unified mass, we stand firm to fix the shattered Humpty Dumptys of our world. We are the people Jesus is counting on to carry out His work in the world. Jesus is our starting point. Our relationship with Him enables us to be who we ought to be. So we dare not take that relationship lightly.

## UNDERSTANDING THE NATURE OF OUR RELATIONSHIP WITH GOD

God takes His relationship with man—particularly His relationship with His people—very seriously. Throughout Scripture the word *covenant* is used to explain God's relationship to His people and the relationship of God's people to one another.

In contemporary terminology, a covenant is similar to a contract.

Both are legally binding agreements between two or more parties. If one party does not fulfill its contractual responsibility, then a court can be called upon to study the contract and uphold it by enforcing the consequences or penalties of breaking the agreement. The same is true of a covenant. However, there is one critical difference between a contract and a covenant. A covenant is more than a contract; it is also a relationship.

It is possible to make a contract with someone you hate. As long as the business side of the contract is beneficial to you, you don't have to like the person with whom you make a contract. But that's not true in a covenantal agreement. In a covenant, the relationship is part of the agreement. You don't have a covenant unless you have a relationship. Marriage is a covenant (Malachi 2:14) because it's more than a legal agreement. The element that makes marriage really marriage is the relationship between the man and woman, not the piece of paper called a marriage license.

In our day, many of us don't realize the all-encompassing, serious nature of a covenant, so we tend to take covenants lightly. If we are to understand our special relationship with God, we must know what the Bible means when it talks about a covenant. I define a covenant as

> a divinely established, legally binding relationship between two or more parties who agree to function under a designated structure of authority in accordance with revealed guidelines, resulting in long-term consequences.

Man's covenantal relationship with God is a fundamental part of human existence. It was part of God's plan even before creation. To understand the biblical significance and meaning of a covenantal relationship, we must look at Genesis 1. After God created the earth and filled it with animals, He said, "Let Us make man in Our image, according to Our likeness; and let them rule over the fish of the sea and over the birds of the sky and over the cattle and over all the earth, and over every creeping thing that creeps on the earth" (Genesis 1:26). This verse captures the essence of man's relationship with God.

Notice that the covenant between God and man began with God. We did not create ourselves. We did not become human beings through some freak accident in the cosmos. God purposely created us and our relationship with Him. God did not create a personal relationship with other aspects of His creation. Only man was created in God's image, so only man can have a personal relationship with God.

Although God created us in His image, we must understand that we are distinct from God; we are not the same as God. God is our creator.

Nothing in the whole universe is like Him. In fact, the universe in its entirety cannot add up to one microscopic element of God's essence. God is a distinct and superior creator.

Despite God's distinction from His creation, He is intricately involved with it. He is not distinct in the sense that He is distant. In fact, Colossians 1:15-17 explains that God not only created the heavens and the earth, He holds it together—He sustains it—even to this day. Thus, God is actively involved in our lives and requires us to respond to Him in every aspect of life. By nature of our creation, we are in relationship with God and are not free to do our own thing.

Our covenant with God is not a static, distant agreement. As our definition says, a covenant is a "*relationship* between two or more parties who agree to *function* under a designated structure of authority in accordance with revealed guidelines." A covenant has a purpose and comes with operating responsibilities, authority, and guidelines. A covenant is to be put into practice. It is a fundamental and inseparable part of life.

In God's original covenant, He gave man the responsibility to care for and rule over the earth (Genesis 1:26). God gave Adam and Eve authority to fulfill their responsibility under the covenant. However, He did not allow them to make up their own rules. The relationship was governed by God's rules only.

Adam and Eve broke the rules God had established for their relationship. The consequences were disastrous. The remainder of Scripture records God's efforts to reestablish His covenant with man. God repeatedly went to great lengths—finally sacrificing His Son—to make a new covenant with His people (1 Corinthians 11:25).

An individual's covenant with God is a powerful agreement. It is an agreement that God means something. It is an agreement that changes how we live. When we accept Jesus Christ as Savior, we agree to allow Him to be Lord of our lives. When we are baptized, we are making a public statement that affirms our covenantal relationship with God. Once we have made an individual covenant with God, we become part of His church. The church is where redeemed people place themselves under God's guidance to live and carry out the ministry of the church.

*If the church is ever going to make an impact on society, it must realize that God makes the rules.* He has given us authority in the earth, but we exercise that authority according to His rules. God has rules for our personal life. He has rules for our family life. He has rules for the church's life. He has rules for society's life. Those rules are to be obeyed. If we ignore God's rules and make up our own, we will face the consequences.

God has established rules for individuals, families, and the church. Escaping those rules is as impossible as escaping the effects of gravity. If you jump out a window, you're going to land on the ground with a thud. There's no way around it. If we obey God, we'll receive blessing; if we disobey God, we'll incur judgment (Galatians 6:7-8).

When we come under God's covenant, we come under His rules. We can't ignore the fact that there is a cause-and-effect relationship between God's rules and our response. Whatever our response, we will reap the effect. If we choose to break His rules, we will break ourselves.

We see evidence of this fact in God's efforts to deliver the people of Israel from Egypt and lead them into the Promised Land. As soon as the people got near the Promised Land, they rebelled against God's rules. God wasn't going to tolerate that, so the Israelites never got to where they were going; they were detoured and spent forty years wandering in the wilderness (Deuteronomy 27-30).

Likewise, the problems we face in our society are the result of individuals, families, churches, and society at large making up new rules rather than following God's rules. For example, the church has failed to teach about sex properly, so society has developed its own sex education program. Society's programs are usually devoid of moral absolutes, so they undermine the family and neglect to teach individual moral responsibility. This faulty teaching has led to an increase in teenage pregnancy, single-parent families, sexually transmitted disease, welfare costs, and perverted crimes. When we abandon God's standards of sexual behavior within the context of heterosexual marriage, all of society suffers. We cannot begin to be what God has created us to be until we accept and commit to obeying God's rules.

We must realize the serious nature of our covenant with God. When we make an agreement with God, we establish a covenant—a legally binding, authoritative agreement that has long-term consequences. The covenantal relationships outlined in Scripture support one another. But when one of those relationships breaks down, when we fail to keep the terms of the covenant, it affects all other relationships as well.

For instance, an individual in covenant with God may raise a family that is also committed to God. All of them become a part of the church, which in turn affects the surrounding community. As each covenantal relationship builds, it benefits the other relationships. But if an individual breaks his or her covenant with God or breaks the marriage covenant, it affects the whole family relationship. When the family relationship is messed up, it will mess up the church, and a messed up church can only help mess up the community. So if we see a messed up community, that often means there are messed up churches, families, and individuals in the community.

God didn't make a covenant for His people to "Amen" and then go on their merry way. He made a covenant to be obeyed. He made a covenant to result in action. The church has no right to do what it wants to do apart from God. As God's people, we are under authority to do what He calls us to do. If we disobey His rules, we effectively cut ourselves off from God and cease to function as the church. Today, the fact that our culture is in such bad shape indicates that many churches have ceased to be the church.

The church is the only institution that can provide long-term benefits in society—the only one. But we must live and minister under God's authority. When the church starts to function according to God's rules, then it will begin to be the redeeming force God intends it to be. Then it will begin to accomplish its task and make an impact on society.

# 7

# The Authority of the Church

The church is a weak and impotent force in society today. It has not defined itself as the group of people through whom God will change the world. The church has not committed itself to being the force that can accomplish God's work in the world. In fact, the church's inability to function as it should can be summed up in its failure to properly respond to Christ's authority.

## JESUS IS LORD OF THE CHURCH

In Colossians 1:16, the Bible tells us that everything was created by Him, through Him, and for Him. This means that the significance of the entire universe can be summed up in its response to the authority of Jesus Christ. Each person's eternal destiny is summed up in his or her response to the person of Christ. A family's ability to live together is summed up in their response to the authority of Jesus Christ. It's the same with the church. Whether or not the church is what it is supposed to be is determined by its response to the authority of Jesus Christ.

Because God initiated His covenant with man, because He established the terms, because He determined the consequences of the relationship, God is in charge of His people. God is the authority over our relationship and how we fulfill the purpose of that relationship over time. He is the boss.

Most of us know what it means to be under someone's authority. When we go to work, supervisors or managers have authority over us. No matter how we feel or what we think about their decisions, we don't have the authority to change them. Instead, we must abide by their decisions because we are under their authority. (Unless, of course, those decisions are repealed by a higher authority.)

As another example, I am the authority in my home. When you walk through my door, you have to abide by my rules. If you smoke, I expect you to refrain while you are in my house. If you drink, you won't do that in my house. If you and your girl friend or boyfriend spend the night in my home, you'll sleep in separate rooms. I don't ask anyone to like those rules, but from the moment you enter my house, you will abide by those rules because I am the authority in my home.

It's the same in the church. Jesus is Lord of the church. We may give verbal assent to that truth, but we often don't like what His lordship means. When we say that Jesus is Lord of the church, that means everyone in the church is to do what He says to do. It doesn't matter whether or not we like what He says to do. It doesn't matter whether we feel like doing what He requires. It doesn't matter if we think we should do something else. When Jesus says to do something, we are under His command to do it.

People like a church that has a good choir. People like a church that has a good preacher. But not nearly as many people like a church where Jesus is truly Lord, because most people want a church where they can do whatever they want; *they* want to be lord. That isn't the way it is in God's church.

Make no mistake about it, God's church was created for Christ. Christ is head of the church: "For by Him all things were created, both in the heavens and on earth, visible and invisible, whether thrones or dominions or rulers or authorities—all things have been created by Him and for Him. . . . He is also head of the body, the church" (Colossians 1:16-18). So the church wasn't created for you. The church wasn't created for me. The church wasn't even created for itself. The church was created for Christ.

As Lord of the church, Christ expects His people to carry out His instructions—to fulfill His purposes. Ephesians 1:23 says that Christ fills the church; He gives the church everything it needs to be and do that which He desires. The life, power, and impact of Christ flows through His church, and it responds by carrying out His agenda in history. The church fulfills His goal of reflecting the reality of God and demonstrating His power.

Christ fills the church with His solutions to poverty, crime, drugs, despair, divorce, immorality, and hate. As the church applies these solutions to itself, it becomes a model of something that works. Society is then blessed by implementing these solutions or cursed for rejecting them. Christ will have clearly made His point through the church. This is why Jesus said, "By this all men will know that you are My disciples, if you have love for one another" (John 13:35). What we do in the church for one another should be so powerful, work so well, and make so much sense that all people will see the power of Christ working in and through His church.

## JESUS HAS ABSOLUTE AUTHORITY OVER SATAN

Throughout history, Satan has struggled to wrest authority from God. Satan wants sovereign control of the universe, but God will not give it to him. Yet Satan never gives up. In fact, he has pulled some pretty smooth moves to eliminate God's authority over His creation.

In the Garden, Satan enticed Adam and Eve to rebel against God. But God countered Satan's move by restoring fellowship with Adam and Eve. Next, Satan prompted Cain to kill Abel in revenge so he could put an end to the godly line. But God countered the move by bringing along Seth, who reestablished the godly line.

Later, Satan got almost every person in the world to rebel against God. Then God called Noah, preserved a remnant of godly people, and wiped out what Satan had ruined. Satan responded again, attempting the ultimate humanistic coup—setting up a one-world government headed by men independent of God. God again countered by confusing their languages, destroying their goals, and decentralizing their program. God then developed His own nationalistic strategy by calling Abraham to be the father of a nation that He would rule.

Satan, not to be outdone, used Pharaoh to oppress God's people. Pharaoh kept God's people from accomplishing God's goals and reflecting God's image to the world. But again God responded. He called Moses out of Midian to serve notice on Pharaoh to let His people go.

Repeatedly, Satan tempted the nation of Israel to rebel against God. Each time, God called a prophet to bring His people back to repentance. Throughout the Old Testament we see Satan finding a way to keep God's program from being successful. But the New Testament brings a new move to the game—a move Satan never anticipated.

In Matthew 1:16, we learn that "to Jacob was born Joseph the husband of Mary, by whom was born Jesus, who is called Christ." God's ultimate countermove to Satan's relentless attack was to become a man. Satan never imagined that God would Himself enter time and space to wage spiritual war.

JESUS HAS AUTHORITY BY BIRTH

Because the man Jesus was also God, He brought ultimate authority to bear on earth. Even so, Jesus was not immune to Satan's attacks. After His baptism, where God personally presented Jesus to the world as His Son (Matthew 3:16-17), Jesus was led into the wilderness to be tempted by Satan (Matthew 4:1).

Jesus didn't go into the wilderness on His own. The Holy Spirit led Him there. So we can assume that it was God's idea for Jesus to take on Satan. I believe the reason God led Jesus to do battle with the devil was to show what Jesus was made of spiritually.

Before He met Satan in the wilderness, Jesus fasted for forty days and forty nights. The purpose of fasting is to give up a craving of the body because the spirit has a greater need. Fasting is saying no to the body's desire because a greater spiritual concern needs attention. Jesus fasted in preparation for the spiritual challenge He knew lay ahead.

Obviously, after fasting for forty days, Jesus was famished. He paid a high price for those days of fasting. He certainly lost weight, and after that long a fast He might even have been in danger of losing His life. That's when Satan made his move (Matthew 4:1-3). Satan came in with a great idea—one I call Operation Breadbasket. He essentially said, "Since You're the Son of God, make it easy on Yourself; turn these stones into bread."

Satan's proposal really wasn't a bad idea. He had a practical, sociological program that met a legitimate human need. He knew Jesus was hungry. He expressed concern about Jesus' problem. He presented a very workable solution. There was only one problem: Satan's solution wasn't God's solution.

JESUS HAS AUTHORITY THROUGH THE WORD

Jesus' response to Satan is significant. He said, "It is written, 'Man shall not live on bread alone, but on every word that proceeds out of the mouth of God' " (Matthew 4:4). From Scripture we know that Jesus is Himself the Living Word. Yet He seized the power of the written Word and used it as a weapon against the enemy. Jesus could have easily said, "I say that man does not live . . ." However, He considered it prudent to use the authority of the written Word against Satan. How much more important is it for us to use the Word against the enemy.

Jesus' quote of Scripture comes from Deuteronomy 8:3. His choice of that quotation to combat Satan's temptation shows that Jesus fully understood the spiritual issue at stake. It shows He knew that our battle is not against flesh and blood but against unseen spiritual powers. Today, our real battle isn't against drugs, teenage pregnancy, poverty, or homelessness. The real issue is discovering the spiritual realities that cause the physical problems.

In His response, Jesus was quoting from the experiences of the Israelites in the wilderness. While they were wandering about, they became hungry and needed God to provide food for them. So God faithfully provided manna six days a week. However, the Israelites didn't just get a feeding program from God; they received a supernatural provision that enabled them to pass through the wilderness. By quoting from this passage of Deuteronomy, Jesus reinforced the fact that everything we deal with on earth has a spiritual cause. He was saying once again that the solutions to physical problems must come from a proper spiritual base.

When he heard Jesus' answer, Satan knew that he had lost another round. But he wasn't ready to give up. We next read (Matthew 4:5-8) that God allowed Satan to take Jesus to the pinnacle of the Temple, where he proposed his next temptation. This time, Satan tried to overcome Jesus by using Jesus' own weapon—Scripture—against him. Satan quoted Scripture to try to get Jesus to follow his agenda rather than God's. "If You are the Son of God," Satan said, "throw Yourself down; for it is written, 'He will give His angels charge concerning You'; and 'On their hands they will bear You up, lest You strike Your foot against a stone' " (Matthew 4:6).

High on the utmost pinnacle of the Temple, Satan came up with a pretty spectacular proposal. He knew that Jesus wanted the Jews to recognize Him as their Messiah. So once again he expressed concern for Jesus' needs. He essentially said, "Let's joint-venture this thing. If You do what I say and jump, Your angels will save You and the Jews will finally recognize that You are the Messiah. With my help, You'll have what God wants for You!"

The scheme didn't work. Jesus knew Scripture better than the devil did. He knew that Satan wasn't telling the full story. So Jesus quoted Scripture again to explain the meaning of the text Satan quoted. In Matthew 4:7, Jesus says, "On the other hand, it is written 'You shall not put the Lord your God to the test.' "

Jesus knew what was written. He knew that Satan's plan wasn't God's plan. He knew that if the objective is to accomplish God's plan, then God's process must be used. God's plan must be accomplished through God's method. The end does not justify the means.

One of the great tragedies of our day is that the church, instead of demonstrating the unique process God uses to accomplish His impact in society, often takes the world's methods, sprinkles a little Jesus on them, and then assumes the agenda is spiritual. Nothing could be further from the truth. God doesn't need Satan to advise His people on how to make an impact. He doesn't need the devil's blessing on our impact in society any more than Jesus needed Satan's help to establish His role as Messiah. God only accomplishes His goals through *His* methods.

Jesus' second response frustrated Satan, but he wasn't ready to quit. Satan next took Jesus to a high mountain and said that if Jesus would worship him, Jesus could have everything He saw (Matthew 4:8-9). Satan put everything out on the table. He finally asked Jesus to do what he wanted Him to do all along. Finally he revealed the real issue—the spiritual issue—which was, "Worship me!"

Notice the progression in Satan's temptation. First, he came out with a food program—not the real issue. Next he came out with a nice-sounding plan for doing God's will—not the real issue. Finally he presented the bottom line—"Worship me!" If Jesus had turned stones into bread, He would have been worshiping Satan. If He had jumped from the Temple, He would have been worshiping Satan. Although turning stones into bread is a good thing, Jesus would have done it at the wrong person's instructions. Although jumping from the Temple pinnacle would have brought Him recognition, Jesus would have done it at the wrong person's instructions. If He had done any of the things Satan suggested, He would have abandoned God's agenda and hopped on Satan's agenda.

For the third time, Jesus refused Satan's agenda. Once again He depended on "It is written" and stayed on track with God's agenda (Matthew 4:10). Then Satan left Jesus, and the angels rushed in and ministered to Him. This battle was over. Jesus had exercised authority over Satan. Satan would try again later, this time for keeps—or so he thought—by getting Christ nailed to the cross. Satan wanted to get rid of Jesus once and for all, but the scheme failed. Jesus demonstrated complete and final victory over Satan by His resurrection from the dead.

JESUS HAS GIVEN HIS AUTHORITY TO THE CHURCH

Jesus has clearly demonstrated His ultimate authority over the earth and the forces of Satan. The amazing thing is that Jesus has given the same authority to the church. Jesus returned to heaven but left the church to stand in His place and to reconcile the world to God. Jesus is Lord over all the earth, but He is Lord through His church.

In our study of Matthew 16:13-17, we learned that discovering who Jesus is is the starting point for the church. Since the disciples were in complete agreement that Jesus was God's Son, Jesus had the group He needed to build His church. Remember what Jesus says about His church in verse 18: "And I also say to you that you are Peter, and upon this rock I will build My church; and the gates of Hades shall not overpower it."

Through this powerful statement Jesus is transferring His power over Satan and the world to His church. Jesus is putting His church on the offensive against Satan. In the church, Jesus has an entity to carry out His authority on earth. Furthermore, Satan cannot overpower Christ's church because Jesus said, "I will give you the keys of the kingdom of heaven; and whatever you shall bind on earth shall be bound in heaven, and whatever you shall loose on earth shall be loosed in heaven" (Matthew 16:19).

Some people have misread this verse to mean that hell is on the *offensive* and the church is on the *defensive*. But this verse isn't talking about hell knocking over the church. It is talking about the church knocking over hell. Jesus isn't just telling us to hang in there and wait for Satan to knock us to the ground and beat us up. He is saying we have what it takes to move forward. He is saying that when His people come together to build His church—based on His word, according to His authority—then hell doesn't have a chance of stopping it.

When I think about the kind of offensive strategy God expects from His church, I think about the San Francisco Forty-niners. They were the team of the eighties. Their greatness was due to their ability to make an offensive impact. They controlled the ball, thereby controlling the game. Their offense was almost always on the field, so other teams rarely had an opportunity to score. Even if the other teams did score, the Forty-niners almost always came back and scored again.

God doesn't expect Satan to "control the ball" in his battle against the church. God expects the church to be on the offensive, executing His game plan. Satan's defense is to be kept on the field while God's offense scores the touchdowns. When Satan's team does have the ball, the church ought to be causing fumbles so the right offense gets back on the field. The church isn't in the game just to keep Satan from scoring. God has called His church to forward-moving Christianity.

Although Jesus has given His authority over Satan to the church, that doesn't mean Satan will leave the church alone. Satan will take any chance he gets to battle God's people, and God allows him to do this. He let Satan take everything from Job—his children, his friends, his wealth, his health—to see if Job would come through with what he said he believed and stand firm for God.

God allows Satan to do the same with us. He allows Satan to take us out on our own, where we don't have our usual support systems to keep us going. God wants to know what we do with all the theology we learn, all the Scripture we memorize, all the good sermons we hear. He wants to know what we do with Him when business is bad and the kids are sick. The only way we find out if we're as spiritual as we think we are is to take on the devil and show what we're made of.

I'm a great basketball player when I'm by myself. The ball goes behind my back, under my legs, and right into the basket. It is impressive to watch me play by myself. But one day Mark Aguirre of the Detroit Pistons came over to the house and wanted to play basketball with me. Suddenly I wasn't good anymore. Every time I went up to shoot, I ate that ball. You see, the way to find out how good I am at basketball is to put me up against six feet, six inches of superstar.

It's the same with us spiritually. We aren't spiritual just because we get excited about a sermon or a song on Sunday morning. Sunday is safe. We're surrounded by people who agree with us. The test of how good we are spiritually comes on Monday morning when we fight it out with the devil in the world. We find out how spiritual we are when we go head-to-head with our unsaved co-workers, when we're sitting in that traffic jam, when we'd like to tell that rude person exactly what we think. That's when we find out how spiritual we are.

## JESUS HAS GIVEN THE CHURCH THE TOOLS OF HIS AUTHORITY

When He returned to heaven, Jesus left the church with the words "I give you my power," thereby giving the church the resources it needed to defeat Satan—the keys of the kingdom of heaven. We studied the keys of the kingdom of heaven in chapter 3 and concluded that, though Satan has many, many schemes to stop the church, Jesus has given us keys to defeat every scheme Satan devises. These keys represent the authority God has given His church to act on His behalf in history to overcome the power of Satan. Heaven backs up the church when we use our keys by applying Scripture to the practical issues of life.

But we have to know where our keys are and what they do. Unfortunately, many of us are guessing about the keys to the kingdom of heaven. We're just guessing about how to live the Christian life. Many churches are just guessing about how to be the church. Many pastors are just guessing about how to lead God's people. Many parents are just guessing about how to raise their children. But while we're guessing, Satan has a field day. Until we learn how to use those keys, Satan has no reason to fear us.

Our keys are God's authority as revealed in His Word. His authority is the doorway to His power. Jesus used God's written Word to defeat Satan. When we apply the Word of God to the power of God, we can also address the problem of sin. Satan has no program, no movement, no challenge that can overcome the church when the church uses the authority of God's Word under His power.

Without Christ, the world cannot begin to stop Satan. He is destroying more of the world every day, and the world has no idea how to stop him. But the church has the power and the authority to clear Satan out of the way. The church has the authority of God's Word. His Word is our key to apply to every problem, whether it be poverty, crime, drugs, single-parent families, or homelessness. We are the ones who can stop hell in its tracks.

However, we must initiate solutions that come from the proper spiritual base. The reason we can't solve our problems is that we apply improper, Satan-inspired solutions instead of God-inspired spiritual solutions. Until we operate under Christ's authority, until the church knows what the keys are and how to use them, we can't offer what the world needs. We must know "it is written" and live by spiritual reality, not by physical reality alone.

## WE CAN FUNCTION ONLY UNDER CHRIST'S AUTHORITY

As God's people, we have tremendous power and authority to solve the problems and heal the wounds of our Satan-oppressed world. However, our authority is a derived authority. Under God's covenant, we do not operate on our own. According to our definition of covenant, we "agree to function under a designated structure of authority in accordance with revealed guidelines." Therefore, we operate exclusively under Christ's authority (John 14:21).

Christians today often struggle with the concept of Jesus' authority and how it works itself out in our lives. We're often uncomfortable with the idea of operating under Jesus' authority because it is bad news for our egos. Clearly, God doesn't care much for our opinion regarding the terms of His covenant. He has very good reasons for requiring His people to operate by His rules.

First, we don't naturally understand God's way of doing things. Isaiah 55:8-9 says that our ways and thoughts are not His ways or thoughts. In fact, God compares the difference between His thoughts and our thoughts to the distance between the heavens and the earth (v. 9).

Second, in His great wisdom, God has already considered all the possibilities and come up with the only solution to every problem. When He tells us what the solutions are, He doesn't need our opinion; He demands our obedience. He has already applied His infinite reason, knowledge, and understanding to the problem. So God doesn't need us to operate as we think we ought; He requires us to operate as He directs.

Scripture gives us an excellent picture of what it means to understand Jesus' authority. In Matthew 8:5-12 a Roman army officer asks Jesus to heal one of his servants. Jesus wasn't near the officer's home, but He offered to travel there to heal the servant. The officer objected:

> Lord, I am not worthy for You to come under my roof, but just say the word, and my servant will be healed. For I, too, am a man under authority, with soldiers under me; and I say to this one, "Go!" and he goes, and to another, "Come!" and he comes, and to my slave, "Do this!" and he does it. (Matthew 8:8-9)

Scripture says that Jesus was amazed by the officer's understanding and faith. The officer recognized Jesus' authority. He understood what it meant to be under authority. He knew that whatever Jesus said would come to pass. He understood that when a person is under another's authority, he or she will do whatever the person in authority dictates. Jesus rightfully expects His church to have the same understanding of authority. He expects the church to respond to His every word.

As God's people, we have all the authority we need to be salt and light to our world. Jesus has given us all we need to accomplish His task. But we must remember that we are people of a covenant. We are a peculiar people who are to do things a different way. We are to walk, talk, act, think, and move according to a different drumbeat—the drumbeat of God's agenda. We are assured of success only when we operate under His authority, according to His Word.

As long as we live *our* way, as long as our families operate *their* own way, as long as the church runs its life according to *its* rules rather than God's rules, Satan will win. Hell is not scared of people. Hell has defeated people millennium after millennium. But Satan can't handle the Word of God. Satan can't handle Jesus. And Satan can't handle the church when Christ is in control.

# 8

# Accountability Within the Church

Many problems in the church today stem from our failure to take seriously God's sovereign authority over us. Jesus has given His church the authority to overcome Satan in the world. However, He has not given the church *independent* authority. The church derives its authority solely from the Lord. Since God is the source of the church's authority, He holds the church accountable to function according to His authority.

Despite our often careless view of His authority, God takes His sovereign role very seriously. In fact, if the church operates apart from His authority, God says He will withdraw His presence, leaving it powerless (Revelation 2:5, 16). A powerless church cannot come up with solutions to the world's problems, cannot keep its members from sin, and cannot impact society as God intends.

The reason for this is obvious. Satan is the spiritual source that empowers the destruction and deterioration of man. Satan's followers are obeying his authority to the max. Therefore, the solutions to counteract Satan's negative spiritual power must—of necessity—be spiritual. To apply those spiritual solutions to life, God's people must obey Him completely. The church is the entity through which God's power will overcome the evil one. But if the church refuses, or resists, God's authority, it automatically rejects His power and destroys its potential for societal impact.

### JESUS: THE JUDGE OF HIS CHURCH

The book of Revelation portrays Jesus as the authority and judge of His church. He is not a distant Jesus, casually enjoying the good times in

75

heaven. He is moving about among His churches, observing and holding each one accountable to obey His rules and fulfill His mission.

The Jesus revealed to John is not soft-skinned and sweet-smiling: "His head and His hair were white like white wool, like snow; and His eyes were like a flame of fire; and His feet were like burnished bronze, when it has been caused to glow in a furnace, and His voice was like the sound of many waters" (Revelation 1:14-15).

I'm afraid most of us have been dealing with the wrong Jesus. We've been relating to a baby-faced Jesus who says, "This is what I'd like you to do, but I understand if you don't want to do it. It's OK if you do what you want to do." The Jesus described in Revelation doesn't stand in the midst of the church to pat it on the back. He stands in the midst of the church to judge it—to tell it where it went wrong and that it had better repent and do what it is supposed to do.

In Revelation 1:12–3:22, Jesus judges His church for specific failures: when it allows right doctrine to become more important than love for Him; when it compromises with the world; when the church doesn't maintain moral purity among its members; when it hides behind its reputation, yet serves Him halfheartedly; when the church has received great blessing, but remains unfaithful to the task God has given; and when the church is too weak to impact the world.

Jesus is not smiling at the way we run our lives. He's not grinning at the way we run our homes. He's not happy about how we run our churches. He has eyes like fire, and if He's that serious about examining and judging His church, you can imagine how angry He is with the world.

### THE PASTOR: HELD ACCOUNTABLE
### TO DELIVER GOD'S MESSAGE

The apostle John's vision from God was to be delivered to all the churches (Revelation 1:11). Specifically, Jesus gave a message of judgment to each pastor, which He expected the pastor to give to the people. Why did He single out pastors to receive the message of judgment? It is because in the New Testament pastors take the place of the Old Testament prophets. Pastors have the responsibility to prophetically deliver God's Word to His people.

God's people need to understand His Word. The pastor's job is to deliver the Lord's message to the whole congregation so everyone can hear what the Lord has to say. As pastor of Oak Cliff Bible Fellowship, I can't present just any message on Sunday morning. When I stand in the pulpit, I am supposed to give *God's* message to the church. I am supposed to explain God's Word to His people. When I stand in the pulpit, what I think doesn't amount to very much. What's important is what God says—what Scripture says. The moment I go beyond what Scripture says and start saying what I think, our church will become a cult.

It is imperative that I give God's message to the church because it is *His* church. Jesus intends to build such a mighty church that hell can do nothing to harm it. Hell can very easily take care of Tony Evans's church. Hell can take care of Chuck Swindoll's, John McArthur's, and E.V. Hill's churches, too. But hell can't do much with Jesus' church. Pastors must be absolutely sure that they are proclaiming *Jesus'* message to His church.

As a pastor of Christ's church, I am accountable to Jesus for the message I deliver to God's people. My responsibility doesn't end there, however. I am also accountable for making sure God's people implement His message through the life of the church. Not every sermon is supposed to make God's people feel good. Some sermons are supposed to make God's people feel miserable and squirm in their seats. Some sermons are supposed to make God's people apologize to one another. Some sermons are supposed to make God's people right the wrongs of their past. Some sermons are supposed to make God's people revamp their lives, agendas, and entertainment habits.

Sermons are to declare the Word of God, and the Word of God is sharper than a two-edged sword (Hebrews 4:16). God's Word cuts and prunes away the worthless, superfluous growth in our lives so that we can bear fruit. When God's Word is at work, it can be mighty uncomfortable, but it will transform us into the dynamic, life-changing people God intends us to be.

## THE CHURCH: THE MEANS BY WHICH GOD HOLDS HIS PEOPLE ACCOUNTABLE

Pastors have great responsibility in God's church, but they can't do the job alone. God's people can hear the greatest sermons every Sunday morning, but that doesn't mean they will implement what they hear. So one of God's purposes for the church is to provide an accountability system for His people.

Agreeing to become part of the church is a serious decision. It is not to be taken lightly. If we say we belong to Jesus, we must participate in His church—the only institution designed to accomplish the will of God in society. To say that we love the Lord but choose not to be a part of His church is contradictory.

To be a member of God's church is to participate in an accountable community of believers who function under the lordship of Christ and are responsible to one another under the guidelines of God's authority. The church holds us accountable to live out our commitment to our covenant with God. It encourages us to live for God and disciplines us when we fail to keep the covenant.

However, the church today has a problem. Many people want to be a part of the church but only if they can play by their own rules. That's not the way the church works. Everyone in the church is accountable to abide by the terms of the covenant—the pastor, the elders, the deacons, the whole congregation. When we become a part of the church—when we come into the covenant—we agree to live by the rules God established long ago as revealed in Scripture.

God's people come under the authority of the church, but the church in turn is accountable to the authority of Scripture. The church doesn't have the authority to tell people where to live, what car to drive, or how many children to have. But the church has everything to say about faithfulness in the marriage relationship, obedience in the parent-child relationship, honesty in financial matters, ethics in business, compassion for the oppressed, the legitimacy of the just use of the death penalty, and the illegitimacy of homosexuality and sex outside of marriage. Those are the issues the Bible addresses, the issues that come under the authority of the covenant.

If the church is ever to fulfill its mission, it must hold God's people accountable to Him. If the saints are not held accountable to live by God's rules, how can the church possibly tell sinners how to live? If the saints—those who are saved and sanctified, and have the Holy Spirit and the Word of God—in the church won't live right, the church has nothing to offer the community at large. The church can't change the community when the church is in chaos.

For this reason, the apostle Peter says, "It is time for judgment to begin with the household of God" (1 Peter 4:17). The church is the starting point for judgment because our society doesn't know how to judge itself. Society has no standards, no criteria for judgment. The church, however, is different. God has already established what is wrong and what is right and revealed it through Scripture. He has said it is wrong to cheat in business. He has said it is wrong to beat your wife. He has said that racism doesn't belong in His church. He has said that sexual purity is important.

God has provided the church with His rules for how we function. We are accountable for our actions to the Lord of the church, who accomplishes His work through us. That accountability is both positive and negative.

Positively, it yields benefits such as the meeting of financial needs (Titus 3:14), spiritual needs (Galatians 6:1), emotional needs (Romans 12:15), and family needs (Titus 2:1-5). Negatively, it means the church has the authority to discipline those who rebel against God's Word (Matthew 18:15-17) and to settle conflicts among church members (1 Corinthians 6:1-11).

## BAPTISM: THE SYMBOL
## OF OUR COMMITMENT TO GOD

Baptism is not just a "get-wet" ceremony; it is a powerful symbol. When we are baptized, we are affirming that we have been raised up into a new way of life—a way of life that rejects immorality, chooses not to give in to the control of drink or drugs, and is no longer governed by our own agenda. When we are baptized, we are making a public statement that we have agreed to live under God's authority through the church.

In the Old Testament, circumcision is the public symbol of covenant with God. Circumcision indicated an agreement to live under God's authority. For God's people today, baptism indicates the same commitment to God's authority.

Before God led the Israelites into the Promised Land, He required that every male be circumcised because it was a statement of commitment (Genesis 17:10-14). He was not going to give the Promised Land to people who were not committed to Him. Under the rules of the covenant, it is impossible to receive God's blessing without first making the commitment God requires.

Part of the problem in the church today is that many people want God's blessing without making a corresponding commitment to Him. They want casual Christianity and abundant blessing. But that isn't how God works. God holds His people accountable to a serious commitment, which then results in abundant blessing. Many people who go to church never experience God's blessing because they never submit to His authority.

If we don't keep our commitment to God, we face serious consequences. We don't just miss out on the blessing; we're in deep trouble. Look what happened to Moses (who certainly should have known better) when he didn't take God's covenant seriously. Moses neglected to circumcise his son. God was so outraged that He was going to kill Moses (Exodus 4:24-26). Moses was spared from God's wrath only because his wife stepped in and circumcised their son. Her action bridged the gap and maintained the family's covenant with God. If we don't take our commitment seriously, God Himself holds us accountable for it.

Whether we realize it or not, God's symbols are powerful. They mean something. We cannot ignore their meaning. While traveling in South America several years ago, I met a twelve-year-old Christian girl who had been put out into the streets by her Muslim family. I assumed that her family had rejected her because she had become a Christian.

"Oh, no," she explained. "They have known for some time that I am a Christian. They did not throw me out until I was baptized!"

Unfortunately, this girl's Muslim family understood the power of baptism more clearly than many Christians. Baptism makes a clear and public statement about who has ultimate authority in our lives. It symbolizes our commitment and accountability to God.

## COMMUNION: THE SYMBOL AND VEHICLE OF PERSONAL ACCOUNTABILITY

Communion continues our commitment to accountability that we established through baptism. Communion is our means of self-examination. It enables us to recognize and deal with our sin before God has to step in and deal with it. It is the vehicle through which we analyze ourselves, come clean with God, and take in spiritual nourishment so that we may live as God's people.

Communion is a serious act that renews our commitment to the covenant. Covenants aren't something we are supposed to commit to once and forget about. God knows that, left on our own, we will forget His covenant—just as Israel did. So He has provided Communion as the process by which we renew the covenant—the process by which we renew our commitment to live under Jesus' authority.

In John 6:53-58, Jesus teaches what it means to take Communion:

> Truly, truly, I say to you, unless you eat the flesh of the Son of Man and drink His blood, you have no life in yourselves.
>
> He who eats My flesh and drinks My blood has eternal life, and I will raise him up on the last day.
>
> For my flesh is true food, and My blood is true drink.
>
> He who eats My flesh and drinks My blood abides in Me, and I in him.
>
> As the living Father sent Me, and I live because of the Father, so he who eats Me, he also shall live because of Me.
>
> This is the bread which came down out of heaven; not as the fathers ate, and died, he who eats this bread shall live forever.

Jesus wasn't literally talking about eating His physical body and drinking His blood. However, the life-giving power of the Spirit that the elements of Communion symbolize is just as real as Jesus' physical body. Jesus was saying that there is real spiritual presence and power in Communion.

When we take the body and blood of Jesus as represented in the elements of Communion, we are feeding ourselves with divine empowerment. We are symbolically refueling our spirits in order to live according to the terms of our covenant with God. Just as we need food to keep us going physically, we need to be fed at the Lord's table so we don't become spiritually weak. The act of Communion fills us with strength to accomplish our spiritual tasks.

Communion is not a boring exercise. It is eating and drinking the power of life. When we became Christians, we appropriated Jesus' flesh and blood for the forgiveness of our sins. In essence, Jesus says, "Don't stop appropriating My flesh and blood that delivered you from sin. Keep on eating, keep on appropriating, so that you will have the power to live as I want you to live."

Communion is a wonderful, powerful symbol. But we dare not take it casually. Communion also holds us accountable to the body and blood of our Lord Jesus. The same blood of Jesus that gives us spiritual life will hold us accountable if we take Communion improperly: "Therefore whoever eats the bread or drinks the cup of the Lord in an unworthy manner, shall be guilty of the body and the blood of the Lord. But let a man examine himself, and so let him eat of the bread and drink of the cup" (1 Corinthians 11:27-28).

Our covenant with God has consequences, and the consequences of improperly partaking of the body and blood of Jesus are great. To take Communion properly, we must examine ourselves. We must confess any rebellion against God's authority in our life. Then the blood of Jesus can cleanse us from our failures and energize us to continue living in obedience to God. However, if we don't use Communion as a time to judge ourselves rightly, if we don't take Communion seriously, Scripture says, "He who eats and drinks, eats and drinks judgment to himself, if he does not judge the body rightly. For this reason many among you are weak and sick, and a number sleep" (1 Corinthians 11:29-30).

Many Christians today are weak and can't handle the weight of life. Many can't handle the weight of marriage or bear the weight of their jobs. Many are just weak and don't know why, so they ask others to pray for them. But many are sick because they haven't gotten their spiritual nutrients. What they need is not prayer but to eat properly from the Lord's table.

### CHURCH DISCIPLINE: THE PROCESS
### OF ACHIEVING ACCOUNTABILITY

If we don't judge ourselves through Communion, we open the door for God to judge us. God demands action. He cannot tolerate sin. He never closes His eyes to sin. If we will not judge ourselves, then He steps in to judge. If we fail to judge ourselves, we show that we don't take Jesus' death on the cross seriously. We show little concern for the price God paid to restore His covenant with us.

If members of God's church have made a public commitment through baptism to live under God's authority and do not abide by God's rules, they must be judged. The church is the institution on earth through which God does His judging. God holds the church accountable to His authority in the same way He holds individuals accountable to His authority.

However, many churches today don't want to make judgments. Some even interpret Scripture to say that we are not to judge others. But that is not the case. The Bible doesn't say not to judge. It says that when you judge, make sure you do it correctly because you will be judged by the same standards (Matthew 7:1-5). The church has no choice but to judge. It is impossible to be a New Testament church without judgment and discipline. Therefore, the church had better know God's standards and methods of judgment.

> And if your brother sins, go and reprove him in private; if he listens to you, you have won your brother.
> But if he does not listen to you, take one or two more with you, so that by the mouth of two or three witnesses every fact may be confirmed.
> And if he refuses to listen to them, tell it to the church; and if he refuses to listen even to the church, let him be to you as a Gentile, and a tax-gatherer. (Matthew 18:15-17)

Notice that the first instruction is to recognize the family relationship between believers. When we "reprove" a brother, we are not condemning a stranger; we're approaching someone we care about.

Second, we are not judging our brother just because he does something we don't like. We're not dealing with personalities or personal preferences. We're dealing with sin, a violation of God's standards as revealed in Scripture.

Third, we are to correct our erring brother as quickly and privately as possible. We don't want someone we care about to continue in sin and later face God's discipline. We want our brother to be aware of his sin and deal with it. Furthermore, we don't tell anyone else about our brother's sin—not even someone else in the church.

We have to deal with our brother's sin quickly and privately because the objective is to encourage him to abandon his sin, not to condemn him. We aren't to go to our brother, saying, "You big dummy! How could you do this?" We are to approach our brother with a spirit that says, "If it weren't for God's grace, I'd be doing the same thing" (Galatians 6:1).

Sometimes we Christians are our own worst enemies. We often kill our wounded instead of nursing them back to health. The purpose of judgment is to *help* our failing brother: to encourage and support him as he deals with sin. The church is to be involved in judgment toward restoration, not judgment for the purpose of hurting its members.

Fourth, if the person is willing to work on his sin, we provide support and keep the matter quiet. But if our brother says, "Stay out of my business, I'm going to do what I want," then it's time to bring in reinforcements.

The reinforcements are witnesses who can confirm the fact of the brother's sin. They are not witnesses of rumors. They are witnesses of fact. They have personally witnessed the sin or can verify that the individual does not intend to deal with the sin. They are witnesses of action or attitude. The witnesses must also realize the seriousness of their responsibility and recognize that they will be judged by the same standards by which they are judging (Matthew 7:1-5).

Fifth, if the brother won't listen to a private witness or two or three witnesses, then—and only then—the matter must be brought before the whole church. By the time the whole church becomes involved, the failing brother has had two chances to deal with the sin.

The purpose of the whole church's becoming involved is restoration. If our brother won't listen to one person and won't listen to two or three people, there's still a chance that he'll listen to one of the remaining members of the church. It is possible that the church can rally around him, get his attention, and help him turn away from sin.

Sixth, there are built-in, long-term consequences to breaking God's rules—our covenant with Him. The degree to which we understand the covenant and live under its authority in our personal and church lives is the degree to which we benefit from the covenant.

If the brother refuses to listen to anyone in the congregation, then the church has to discipline him. The church has the authority and responsibility to shut him out. That's hard. It's hard to shut out a brother. But the church has no more options. The brother has already been talked to by one, two, three individuals and even the entire church, yet he persists in sin. So he has to be cast out from God's protection.

What does it mean to cast out a rebellious, sinning member? It means the church members no longer associate with that brother (1 Corinthians 5:11). Church members can no longer have any interpersonal connection with the person until he decides to repent.

God requires such strict discipline because our relationship with Him is based on the covenant—a binding relationship. When a person rebels against Jesus, he can't associate with His children. For example, if you hate my wife, you can't expect to have fellowship with me. By hating my wife, you have also made a decision about me. The connection between parties in a covenantal relationship is unavoidable.

If we have any desire to become the people and the church God intends us to be, if we have any hope of touching our society, we must understand that the church is an accountable membership. We cannot live any way we choose. Although no one can be saved by keeping God's guidelines, our covenant with God is possible because Jesus already kept the guidelines. Jesus already obeyed God's rules by paying for our sins with His life. The consequence of His obedience is that all of mankind can once again have a relationship with God.

In turn, our binding relationship with God brings us under the authority of Christ. Jesus is our new authority, and the local church is His means of authority. Therefore church is not a place where we come and do our own thing. It is where we come to do God's thing. It is where another person has the right to tell us if we're not doing God's thing. If we don't want to be accountable to the authority of the church, then we don't want church—we want a social club, and social clubs can't change society.

When the church operates like a club, there are serious consequences. We see them all around us every day: death, disorder, and destruction. But when the church operates as God's church, when it operates according to God's rules, we will see very different consequences. We will see mended families, rehabilitated drug and alcohol addicts, poverty turned into productivity, decreased racial tension, and a healthy respect for authority. Most important, men and women will come into a personal knowledge of God through Jesus Christ, which is precisely why all social impact must have evangelism at its heart.

# 9

# The Purpose of the Church

God has always had a chosen people—a royal priesthood—whose responsibility it is to fulfill His work on earth. The priesthood is to protect and reveal that which belongs to God so that the world can see what He is like.

In the Garden of Eden, Adam was responsible to guard and maintain the Garden according to God's regulations. God chose Adam as the man to reveal Himself to the world. However, Adam rebelled against God's authority. So God had to remove him from the priesthood and throw him out of the Garden. Then God appointed two angels to guard the Garden in Adam's absence.

God next called Abraham to be the father of His chosen people. Through Abraham, God built a nation that was to be His salt and light in the world. Abraham's descendants became the nation of Israel. Israel's sole purpose was to be God's royal priesthood that would demonstrate His glory to the surrounding nations (Exodus 19:5-6).

God placed Himself at the center point of the lives of His people. The location of the Tabernacle (and later the Temple) in the center of the Israelites' encampment symbolized God's central position in their lives. God made Israel's role and purpose clear: "Now then, if you will indeed obey My voice and keep My covenant, then you shall be My own possession among all the peoples, for all the earth is Mine; and you shall be to Me a kingdom of priests and a holy nation" (Exodus 19:5-6).

It was a great plan, but a problem developed: Israel abandoned the priesthood. Instead of being God's salt and light among the nations, Israel wanted to be like the nations. Instead of guarding that which belonged to God, Israel carelessly tossed it aside. Once again, the world was without God's effective royal priesthood, which eliminated the evidence of God's presence in the world.

When Israel reneged on its opportunity to be God's holy nation, God did not give up on His royal priesthood. Instead, He set Israel aside for a time and selected a new group of people to represent Him in the world. While on earth, Jesus announced the change in the priesthood: "Therefore I say to you, the kingdom of God will be taken away from you, and be given to a nation producing the fruit of it" (Matthew 21:43).

This new group of people is the church. Until God reestablishes His program with Israel, He has selected a new group of people made up of Jews and Gentiles grafted into one body, who are to reflect God's character in history. So God's plan for a royal priesthood remains the same; only the group of people He has chosen is different (Romans 11).

Peter beautifully portrays what it means for the church to be God's chosen priesthood:

> But you are a chosen race, a royal priesthood, a holy nation, a people for God's own possession, that you may proclaim the excellencies of Him who has called you out of darkness into His marvelous light; for you once were not a people, but now you are the people of God. (1 Peter 2:9-10)

God didn't choose the church to make us feel good. He chose us purposefully, with an agenda in mind. We are God's possession. Our agenda is to proclaim the excellencies of His marvelous light to the world. The church is the army God established on earth to recapture that which has been in the hands of the enemy and turn it over to the dominion of Jesus Christ. Our purpose in life is to proclaim God's glory. We are God's chosen people, called to display His glory throughout the earth.

The church is not just programs and structures. The church is a people with a purpose—a people with a ministry. Being part of the church, therefore, means to breathe the life of God into whatever we touch and whatever we do. The ministry of the new priesthood is to live according to God's authority, thereby showing the world what God is like.

## WHAT IS THE MINISTRY OF THE CHURCH?

God relates all things in heaven and on earth to Jesus (Ephesians 1:10). To put it another way, God measures everything by its relationship to Jesus Christ. On judgment day, God will not ask how many sins we have committed. He will, however, want to know all about our relationship to Jesus Christ. That which is related to Jesus will stand. That which is not related to Jesus will be discarded. So the job of the church—the people who are related to Jesus Christ—is to show the world what life looks like when it's properly related to Jesus. Thus, every aspect of our lives ought to relate to Jesus. That which doesn't relate to Jesus ought not to be in our lives.

What does this mean to practical, everyday living? What we watch on television ought to be acceptable to Jesus, or we shouldn't watch it. The music we listen to ought to be acceptable to Jesus, or we shouldn't listen to it. Our wardrobe ought to be acceptable to Jesus, or we shouldn't wear it. They way we handle our work and career ought to be acceptable to Jesus, or we should make changes. The way we drive our cars ought to be acceptable to Jesus, or we should change our driving habits. Our recreation ought to be acceptable to Jesus, or we should change what we do. Our performance in school ought to be acceptable to Jesus, or we should set new standards.

The church's ministry is to lead the way in relating all aspects of life to Jesus. The church ought to lead the way in showing the world how Jesus would live if He were on earth, doing what we do. Not only must our lifestyle reflect Jesus to the world, but the way we approach society's problems must reflect Jesus too.

We need to make a fundamental distinction between the way Christians and non-Christians impact society: "Let your light shine before men in such a way that they may see your good works, and glorify your Father who is in heaven" (Matthew 5:16). When God says that our light is to shine "in such a way," He means that there are definitive guidelines as to how He wants His work accomplished.

He wants His work done in two specific ways. First, He wants it done so that men see our good works. There is to be a visible demonstration of our faith in society. Second, our good *works* are not simply good *things*. Non-Christians can do good things such as building hospitals and orphanages. They can feed the poor and clothe the naked. But they can't do good *works*. Paul describes good works in Ephesians 2:10, when he says that we are created in Christ "*for good works, which God prepared beforehand, that we should walk in them*" (italics added). Good works are God's works. Good works are biblical goals accomplished through biblical methods. It's not enough to have good goals; they must be accomplished God's way.

We know our social action is done God's way when it glorifies our Father in heaven (Matthew 5:16). God always gets the credit for His good works. He does not get the credit for good *things*. Thus, the church feeds the poor so it can share the gospel. The church creates adoption services so it can reflect God's hatred of abortion. The church shelters the homeless so it can offer an eternal home. The church establishes restitution to teach the biblical significance of work and responsibility. The church counsels addicts to demonstrate the freedom of life in Christ.

Such a visible display of God's glory will affect how others view our social-action programs. It may lessen the amount of government grants we receive. It may make people think we are proselytizing. It may make others think of us as fanatics. However, doing good works in a way that displays God's glory is the only kind of social action God approves. Anytime we hide our commitment to God to carry out our programs, we lose God's support for our agenda. God's concern is that His will be done and His kingdom come so that His glory is visibly displayed.

Being God's royal priests in a hurting world is an awesome responsibility that involves every aspect of life. Many of us don't want to take our ministry that seriously. We find it easy to dismiss the importance of our ministry, which makes it easier to choose not to minister. But ministry is important to God. We are on earth to carry out His program. We are His holy priests, who are to show the world what Jesus would be like if He were here. If God didn't need us to minister on earth—to use His power to address the world's needs—He would have taken us to heaven the moment we became Christians. The reason we are still on earth is because we have some serving to do; we are to be doing the work of ministry.

As God's people, we must realize the great significance of our ministry. Paul wrote, "I pray that the eyes of your heart may be enlightened, so that you may know what is the hope of His calling, what are the riches of the glory of His inheritance in the saints" (Ephesians 1:18). Why does he pray in this way for the church? He knows it's easy for us to lose our perspective. He knows it's easy for us to lose our vision for ministry. He knows it's easy for us to live defeated Christian lives. So he prays that we might know what we're all about—that we might know our ministry and pursue it with enlightened spirits.

## ALL ARE TO MINISTER

Many Christians don't really know what the ministry of the church is all about. Some think that showing up in church on Sunday morning is ministry. Some think that the pastor and the church staff are the ones who minister. These conceptions are absolutely wrong. If God's people are to have a proper view of ministry, they have to overcome these misconceptions.

The church staff alone is not responsible to do the ministry of the church. Every believer is supposed to do the work of ministry through the church. No one is to be on the sidelines. Everyone who is part of the church is to do the work of ministry. None are exempt.

At the church where I serve as senior pastor, people cannot join unless they agree to serve. Each prospective member has more than 115 ministry opportunities to choose from—everything from being a parking-lot attendant to tutoring kids to teaching computer skills. The church is a family, so no member of God's household should be allowed to reap the benefits of membership without incurring responsibility to the church that ministers to them.

When I was much younger, I once made the mistake of thinking I didn't have a responsibility to help out in my family. At the time, I was going to school and enduring two football practices a day. When I got home, I was tired. I told my mother that I was too tired to do the chores she wanted me to do. She promptly let me know that if being tired was a legitimate excuse for not fulfilling family responsibilities, she wouldn't have made any meals that day, washed any clothes that day, or cleaned any floors that day. And, if I knew what was good for me, I'd better do my chores and stop the "tired" nonsense.

Just as no parent should allow a member of the family to enjoy the benefits of the family without incurring responsibilities that enhance the family, no member of the church should be allowed to ignore his or her ministry responsibilities in the church. Serving in the church is at the heart of what it means to be a member of the church. This point is so vital to the ministry of the church that our national ministry, The Urban Alternative, devotes significant time to training pastors in the responsibility and accountability of church members.

Make no mistake, the ministry of the church is hard work. We like to sit on the sidelines and direct the ministry of the church, but God calls us to roll up our sleeves and *do* the work of ministry. It's easy to say sing in the choir when we're not in it. It's easy to say the children need more church programs when someone else is working to make the program happen. It's not so easy to get tired, sweaty, and dirty while we play the game, but that's what it means to minister for God's kingdom.

Far too often, church members are like spectators watching a football game. Sixty-thousand people, desperately in need of exercise, sit and analyze twenty-two men on the field who are in great shape. It's easy to critique and review the play on the field when you're sitting with popcorn in one hand and a COKE® in the other. Your perspective changes, however, when you get down where the action is and let the enemy beat on you for a while.

To understand why everyone in the church must do the work of ministry, we must remember how the church functions: the same way our bodies function (Romans 12:5; 1 Corinthians 12:12-27). If we want to understand how the *church* works, we must understand how our *bodies* work.

The head controls every part of the body. The brain tells the rest of the body what to do. Every action of the body is a result of an instruction from the head. The body has a central nervous system—an electrical message system—that communicates the word from the brain to the rest of the body. If we're healthy, and our brain decides to move our hand, the nervous system carries the message to the muscles in the hand and the hand moves.

There's no guarantee that the body will always be healthy. Sometimes a problem develops. If the head is injured, the damaged brain may not be able to tell the body what to do. If the central nervous system is damaged, the brain may tell the hand to do something, but the foot may get the message intended for the hand. Conversely, if parts of the body are injured, they may not be able to fulfill the instructions of the head and nervous system.

Since the church is a spiritual body, it works in a similar way. Jesus is the head of the church. He is the brain. He tells the church what to do. But there's a problem in the body: often the church (the body) doesn't do what Jesus tells it to do. What is the problem?

There's obviously nothing wrong with the *head* of the church. Jesus is alive and well. He's not coming up with wild ideas; He's thinking straight. Our *central nervous system*, the Holy Spirit, is also fine. The Spirit is taking the Word and sending it through the body so the body knows what to do and has the power to do it. The problem lies in the *body*. The hands get the word from the Spirit, but they don't feel like moving. The feet don't feel like walking. The mouth doesn't feel like talking. As a result, the church stumbles around like a diseased body. Think of the message a sick church gives to the world.

When the church rebels against Jesus, its head, the world cannot see what life is like under Jesus' authority. When the church rebels, the world sees that the head says one thing, but the body does another. That isn't how the church fulfills its purpose in the world. What we do, where we go, and what we say show what we think. The world is supposed to be able to look at what the church is saying and doing and know what is on Jesus' mind. If the church isn't doing anything, going anywhere, or saying anything, or if it is doing the wrong thing, going the wrong direction, or saying the wrong thing, then Jesus looks pretty bad. If parts of the body aren't at work in the world, the world has no opportunity to see Jesus.

God has called every member of His church, every part of the body, to reflect Jesus in all areas of life. That's what ministry is all about. Ministry is something every one of us can and must do. There's no excuse for any part of the body not to minister.

Some of us like to think we aren't qualified to minister. But that is no excuse; everyone is qualified: "But to each one is given the manifestation of the Spirit for the common good" (1 Corinthians 12:7). Each one of us has spiritual gifts. Jesus hasn't given us a ministry to accomplish without equipping us to minister. He has given each person the gifts needed to minister in the church (Ephesians 4:7).

We can never say that some Christians are ministers and some are not. It is true to say that some are pastors, prophets, or evangelists, and some are not (Ephesians 4:11). But it is false to say that some are not ministers. The apostle Paul develops this idea further in 1 Corinthians 12:25: "There should be no division in the body, but . . . the members should have the same care for one another." So there's no such thing as ministers and non-ministers in God's church. Ministry isn't just what the pastor does; ministry is what every member does in and through the church.

If anyone in the church decides not to be involved in ministry, it affects the ministry of the whole church. First Corinthians 12:7 clearly states that our spiritual gifts are not for our personal benefit; they are for the benefit of the body. If we refuse to use our gifts for the body, then we're harming the body and the ministry of the church. When a part of the body doesn't work well, it hinders the progress of the entire body.

For instance, when a foot isn't working properly, the body doesn't walk as well. Depending upon the nature of the foot's problem, the body may still be able to walk, but it will not go as far or as fast as it would if both feet were working as they should. In the same way, when a part of the church isn't working properly, the entire church is hindered from accomplishing God's work in the world.

The Bible makes clear that God is pleased when His people minister to one another and to a hurting world. Let Him see His people excited about a *ministry* program instead of a *building* program. Let Him see His people excited about serving. Let Him see His people display His light to a dark world. God is excited when His people are involved in ministry. When His people minister, His priesthood is working.

If ministry is so important to God, it's difficult to understand why it is so hard to get His people to do the work of ministry. Some of us say we can't get involved in the ministry of the church because we "don't have time." That's nonsense! If we don't have time to be involved in the ministry of the church, we've missed out on what God has called us to do. If we don't have time to do the work of ministry, we don't understand the vital importance of God's people showing His stuff to the world.

Some of us don't get involved because we say God hasn't given us anything to do or we don't have any abilities that God can use. As we saw earlier, God has a task for every part of the body. We can't say that God forgot to give us credentials for service when He made us. The problem is not that we can't serve; the problem is that we don't *want* to serve.

Many of us say that God is our everything, yet He can't get anything out of us. Many of us say that God has been good to us, yet we don't seem to have any time to serve the God who is good. Some of say that God has brought us a mighty long way, yet we're moving so fast that He can't catch up with us. Some of say that God is our bridge over troubled water, but when we get to the other side we blow up the bridge.

God had given us abilities for spiritual purposes, not just to generate income. He has given us resources for spiritual purposes, not just to make us comfortable. A car that God can never use to pick up people for church is a misused vehicle. A home that God can never use to serve His saints is a misused home. Money that God has provided that can never be used in His ministry is misused money. God has equipped us with abilities and resources for a purpose—to display the glory of His kingdom to the world.

It is hypocrisy to say that we love God when we don't have time for Him or refuse to serve Him. It is hypocrisy to say that God has been good to us when we won't allow Him to use what He has given us. The better God has been to us, the more thankful we ought to be and the more service we ought to give.

## MINISTRY TOUCHES EVERY ASPECT OF LIFE

By now it ought to be clear that going to church on Sunday morning isn't what ministry is all about. Sunday morning is just the classroom. Going to church merely prepares us for ministry. We go to church to get data about the ministry we are to do when we walk out of the church building and into the world.

We live in a world that places nothing under the lordship of Christ. Sunday reorients us so we can place everything under His lordship and fulfill our purpose all week long. Our purpose for being in church is to find out from our Lord what He wants from us so we can live Monday through Saturday placing all things under His lordship.

The test of a church is the scope of its ministry. Our ministry is to carry Jesus Christ everywhere because we include Him in everything. Everything we touch, He touches. Everywhere we go, He goes. Everything we do, He does. That is why the ministry of the church encompasses all of life. Too often ministry is limited to the narrow scope of singing in the choir, teaching Sunday school, or serving as an usher. These areas of ministry are indispensable but are only a small part of what God has called His people to do.

God has called us to influence and impact (minister to) every area of life. No corner of the world is to be exempt from the ministry of the church. Thus, the church must begin to teach people how God desires them to use their skills and careers to promote God's will and extend His kingdom, not just to bring home a paycheck.

If you're a lawyer, Jesus should be impacting the courtroom and bar association because you're there. If you're a nurse, Jesus should be impacting the hospital. If you're a teacher, Jesus should be impacting the classroom. If you're a laborer, Jesus should be impacting the factory. If you're a mother, Jesus should be impacting the life direction of your children. If you're a father, Jesus should be impacting life-style standards you set for your family. If you're a business owner, Jesus should be impacting how you balance the books. The skills of God's people should also be used to benefit the church to such an extent that they overflow into society (Ephesians 4:11-16).

God created His church so that everything in heaven and on earth would be brought under the lordship of Christ: "And He put all things in subjection under His feet, and gave Him as head over all things to the church" (Ephesians 1:22). Think about that for a minute. Jesus is Lord over all things *through the church*. That means the ministry of the church includes all things.

When we look at the world, it doesn't seem like Jesus is Lord. Wars are going on throughout the world. People suffer from horrible diseases. Powerful people take from others and oppress the less powerful. Children suffer from unthinkable abuse. Millions have inadequate shelter and insufficient food to survive. *How can Jesus possibly be in charge of this mess?* we wonder. It looks like a contradiction. Jesus is over the world and everything in it, but the world doesn't look the way we'd expect Jesus to make it look. What's the problem?

The problem is not just the sinfulness of the sinners. The problem is also the church. The reason everything doesn't look like it's under the lordship of Christ is because His *church* isn't under His lordship. Therefore, nothing else comes under His lordship. The only way the world can see that Jesus is Lord is when the church starts living under the lordship of Jesus in every aspect of life. As the church comes under His lordship, things on earth will come under His lordship. Until the church comprehensively applies the lordship of Jesus to every part of life and every aspect of society, the world will not see Jesus as Lord.

Does this mean that, if the church becomes what God has called it to be, all these problems will disappear? Absolutely not! Even when Jesus was on earth, they didn't disappear. What it does mean is that the world will have a crystal-clear model of what biblical solutions look like. The church will become the pacesetter that the world emulates rather than simply the imitator of secular society's agenda.

The church has a twofold effect on the world: we proclaim life as well as death (2 Corinthians 2:15-16). When the world responds to the message and methods of God as demonstrated through the church, it receives life and access to solutions that work. When it rejects our divine message and methods, then it accepts death and defeat. Either way, God's program and solutions have been clearly revealed.

Some Christians who believe in the imminent return of Jesus Christ argue against social action, saying that "the world getting worse and worse and will ultimately be destroyed. So why spend time polishing the brass of a sinking ship?" My answer is simple: "The same reason we jog even through we're going to die!"

The reality and eventuality of death should increase rather than lessen our health maintenance. Likewise, the hopelessness of our world should increase our impact on it, not decrease it. It could be another 2,000 years before Jesus comes; we can't let our generation self-destruct in the meantime.

Our culture is collapsing because God's priests are not doing the work of ministry in the world. Therefore, the people who are to be revealing God's likeness to the world cannot be seen by the world. As God's people, we must rediscover our priesthood. Everywhere we go and everything we do should show the glory of Jesus to the world. When people meet us, they should meet Jesus. The only way the world will ever see what Christ looks like is when His people are everywhere in the world, living life totally under His authority.

# 10

# The Goal of the Church

Satisfied with more numbers, more money, and more facilities, many churches in America have denigrated, and sometimes altogether missed out on, their primary mission. To put it simply, we are operating on *our* agenda rather than on God's and, therefore, have a lot of religious activity but little impact. If we do not operate on God's agenda, we cannot experience God's results.

As God's people, we have a job to do. Both individually and corporately we have a mission to perform. Jesus did not leave us with vague ideas about what we are to do. Instead, He gave us specific instructions on how to accomplish our mission. While He was on earth, He gathered His disciples together and gave them a vision of what His church is to accomplish. He gave the church a mission. Jesus presents that mission in Matthew 28:19-20, which is what we call the "Great Commission":

> Go therefore and make disciples of all the nations, baptizing them in the name of the Father, and the Son and the Holy Spirit, teaching them to observe all that I commanded you; and lo, I am with you always, even to the end of the age.

Before giving instructions on the mission of the church, Jesus gave His disciples the authority to carry out their mission. Clearly such a mission requires supernatural power to accomplish, and Jesus provides that power. He told His disciples that He possessed all authority in heaven and on earth

(Matthew 28:18) and that His disciples would also have authority to carry out His agenda.

The word Jesus used for authority meant *legitimate, rightful* authority. By choosing that word, Jesus was saying that any attempt to stop His impact on the world was illegitimate. He alone has all legitimate authority in the universe. He has beaten death, Satan's greatest weapon, so no one can lay claim to His sovereign rule.

In a football game, the power of big, strong, muscular men is ruled by a man with a striped shirt and a whistle. The referee alone has ultimate authority in the game. He alone has the power to stop the game and even throw rebellious players off the field. That's the type of authority Jesus claims for Himself. In spite of Satan's attempts to control the universe and the affairs of men, Jesus wears the striped shirt and carries the whistle. He controls the field of play. If we are going to accomplish His mission, we must operate according to His authority.

The mission of the church is to multiply disciples throughout the world—to touch every corner of the world with God's presence. That is an awesome vision. Jesus understood the magnitude of what He was saying, so He didn't just leave us with the vision. He also told us how to make disciples—by going, baptizing, and teaching.

## MAKING DISCIPLES

In the Great Commission, Jesus presented disciplemaking as the goal and mission of church ministry. The church is to make disciples who will go into all the world and touch every aspect of life with God's image and presence. Why is it so important for the church to make disciples? Disciples are people who have committed themselves to living totally under the lordship of Christ in every aspect of life. They are spiritual people. They are the ones—the only ones—who can make the spiritual impact God desires in the world.

Please notice that Jesus didn't say anything about making church members. He didn't say anything about making church buildings. He didn't say anything about making church programs. He said, "Make disciples." One reason the church lacks an effective ministry in our society is because it has been adding numbers but hasn't been making disciples. As a result, spiritual people aren't available to make God's presence known in the world.

The problem in our society is not that we don't have enough money. It isn't that we don't have enough government programs. It isn't that we don't have any sociological answers. The problem is there aren't enough disciples—men and women who understand that their purpose in life is to represent God's kingdom on earth.

We have plenty of church buildings, church members, and church programs. But where are the disciples who are committed to carry out God's program? Where are the disciples who will surrender their existence to the will of God, no matter what the price? We don't need more church members. We need more *disciples*.

One reason we don't have disciples is because making disciples is hard work. Disciples aren't born; they have to be made. Disciples aren't the result of a few good sermons, a Sunday school class or two, or even a weekly Bible study. Disciples are the result of a committed, all-encompassing ministry that provides the knowledge and incentive to live in conformity to Christ. That's why Jesus gave the church a vision for disciplemaking.

When the army accepts a recruit, it doesn't assume that he or she is all the army needs. So the army puts each recruit on a strict training program to conform him to the image of the American soldier and to enable him to accomplish the task given to him. The training process begins when a recruit goes to boot camp. That's where the conformity—the disciple-making, if you will—begins.

From morning until night, the young recruit belongs to Uncle Sam. Uncle Sam tells him when to get up, what to wear, when and what to eat, how to exercise, and what work to do. It doesn't matter if the recruit used to sleep in, wear three-piece suits, dine at the finest restaurants, or relax in the pool. Uncle Sam has complete control. When the training process is over, the young man is sent where the country needs him to serve. It may even be necessary for the young man to give up his life in service to his country.

Now that's what I call a disciple. Lest you think I carried the illustration a bit too far, remember Jesus' words: "If anyone comes to Me, and does not hate his own father and mother and wife and children and brothers and sisters, yes, and even his own life, he cannot be My disciple" (Luke 14:26). Jesus demands our allegiance above any other commitment in life—even life itself. That's what it means to be His disciple.

Many people who call themselves Christians are not really disciples. They may fit in the "nod to God" crowd that shows up on Sunday morning, but they're not disciples. They may want to be tantalized by an entertaining sermon, but they don't want marching orders. Disciples don't naturally occur in this world; they have to be made.

## THE MEANS OF DISCIPLESHIP

Jesus used these participles: going, baptizing, and teaching, to explain the means by which disciples are made.

GO INTO THE WORLD

His first instruction for disciplemaking is for the church to go out into the world. "Go!" That's a tough command for many of us. We've become very comfortable huddled up inside the four walls of the church. But we don't make disciples when we're sheltered within the security of a Sunday morning service. We make disciples when we're out in the marketplace.

The Bible never tells us to bring our non-Christian friends to church so they can become Christians. The Bible says we are to be God's witnesses *out in the world*. We are to go out to the non-Christians and be witnesses on their turf. We are to go out and apply God's Word to every situation we come up against as we live in the world. Then, and only then, will we be salt and light to the world.

The church is where we receive our instructions on how to bring God's solutions to the issues of our day. Unfortunately the church is often a retreat from the world rather than preparation for impacting the world. Just as we stop at gas stations to refuel so that we can continue down the highway, the church refuels the believer to go back into the world, filled with God's power, righteousness, and biblical solutions. No driver would be satisfied to sit at the pump and enjoy the feeling of having a car full of fuel. In the same way, no Christian should be satisfied to simply be filled with the beauty and glory of God's Word and His people. Unless that filling leads us to go into the world and use the Word to impact culture, the purpose of the experience is lost.

It is time we brought a divine frame of reference to our society by being Christ's disciples—uncompromising, dedicated, biblically astute Christians whose goal in life is to live every part of life for the glory of God. As God's people, we carry out God's frame of reference in church, but then it must overflow into all of society so that the world can be exposed to Christ.

IDENTIFY DISCIPLES WITH CHRIST

Second, Jesus says to identify new believers with God through baptism. Baptism in the Bible is used to mean identification (1 Corinthians 10:1-2; Romans 6:3-4). The relationship between water baptism and spiritual baptism is similar to the relationship of a wedding to a wedding ring. The ring doesn't marry you, but it clearly identifies the wearer as one who is married. The ring identifies one who has made a total, lifelong commitment to another person.

Baptism, then, identifies us with Christ's death on the cross and His resurrection into new life. This identification is not only with Christ but also in the name of the Father and Holy Spirit. This is significant because it shows that our lives are to be totally encompassed by the triune God.

That's why Paul says that whether we eat or drink or whatever we do to do it all to the glory of God (1 Corinthians 10:31). Every area of life is sacred and is designed to make God look good and reflect His character, thus revealing our identity with Him. That's what Jesus was explaining to His disciples when He was teaching them how to pray. He explained that the issue of prayer was God's name, God's kingdom, and God's will—not our own name, kingdom, or will. Such is the mind-set and life perspective of a disciple. It is promoting God's character (name), serving God's agenda (kingdom), and using God's methods (will).

Baptism is a public statement of our commitment to God's lordship in every area of life. As we learned earlier, baptism sets the groundwork for accountability in the church. Accountability as symbolized through baptism is necessary to the making of disciples. Disciples cannot be made without accountability that produces obedience to God.

TEACH DISCIPLES HOW TO LIVE

Jesus' next instruction is for the church to teach the disciples. Please notice that teaching comes after baptism. If people are not identified with Christ, they won't slow down long enough to be taught, which explains why more Christians attend music concerts than Bible studies. Unless Christ is our top priority, other activities will always take precedence over learning about Him.

Although it is not the first step in fulfilling the church's mission, teaching is essential. To provide long-term solutions to the world's problems, God's people must address the fundamental spiritual causes of those problems. So we must be spiritually minded and know what the Bible says. Such knowledge comes primarily through teaching. God's people must be taught the spiritual principles revealed through Scripture so that we can apply those principles and develop spiritual solutions to the world's problems.

God has assigned the preacher to teach His people. The preacher is responsible to take God's truth, given many centuries ago, and present it in relevant terms to God's people today. Unfortunately, much of the preaching we hear today has little to do with the Bible. Much of the preaching we hear is not biblical because it doesn't expose God's agenda. Biblical preaching is expository preaching; it is preaching that reaches down into who God is and what He says, and presents God's message in a way we can relate to, understand, and relevantly apply.

It's tempting for the preacher, in order to be relevant, to preach about social agendas, political platforms, and contemporary trends, but that is not his job. Paul gave Timothy what he called a very serious instruction: "Preach the word; be ready in season and out of season; reprove, rebuke, exhort, with great patience and instruction" (2 Timothy 4:2).

Paul didn't say to preach politics, sociology, or economics. His instruction was to preach the Word. God's people need to know that Scripture provides comprehensive data on every life issue. They need to know that Scripture deals with all the sociological circumstances and problems of our day. And, if the preacher preaches God's Word properly, he will be preaching *biblical* sociology, politics, and economics, because the Word deals with each of those issues. No issue stands outside the realm of Scripture.

The job of the preacher is to preach God's Word with integrity. If the preacher relates what God hasn't said, he is not being true to the Bible. If he doesn't present God's Word in a way we can understand, he's not being true to God's people. The preacher must be true to both the Bible and man's contemporary situation.

The preacher must recognize that God's Word doesn't merely relate information. The Bible is inspired. It breathes actualization. That's why Jesus said to teach "them to observe." The preacher doesn't teach just to impart knowledge; he preaches so that the people will observe, understand, and practice the Word of God in life.

Therefore, preaching is never passive. As God's people, we are vitally involved in the message, because the message calls us to action. The preacher not only gives information but helps us apply God's truth to our lives. When he is finished preaching, we should have no doubt that we have heard a message from God and that we need to act in response to that message. When the preacher brings God's Word to the people, exciting things should happen.

Part of the mission of the church is to call God's people to action. God's kingdom can't depend on uncommitted volunteers; they're too busy enjoying themselves to get involved in God's action. So the job of the professional minister, Bible study leader, and Sunday school teacher is to inform and inspire God's people to do His work. Otherwise, God's people get used to enjoying the blessing and neglect their job of going and making disciples.

## DISCIPLES FULFILL THE CHURCH'S MISSION

Once disciples have been made, they aren't difficult to recognize. They are the people who are being inconvenienced for the kingdom, the ones who are paying a price for the kingdom, the ones who are impacting society for God. Disciples have a distinctive life-style that is worthy of their calling.

*Disciples live differently* (Ephesians 4:17). They don't live the same way the world lives. Disciples' lives are qualitatively different. They are not different for the sake of eccentricity; they are different because they walk to the beat of a different drummer. Disciples walk according to divine instructions, divine guidelines, and divine ethics. Disciples walk on earth but think like heaven. They live heavenly lives in a hellish world.

*Disciples live in love.* They live in service to God, which makes them willing to sacrifice their personal goals and comfort for the betterment of others. The Bible says that disciples ought to love one another so much that they would give their lives for one another (John 13:34-35). But very few Christians are actually willing to do that because they don't know what love means. We aren't willing to serve one another in the church because we don't love as God wants us to love. Yet God says that the way we love one another shows how much we love God.

Ephesians 5:8 says that *disciples live as children of light.* That means they live in a way that is pleasing to the Lord. That means they are constantly in the Word of God—to discover His will and live accordingly. As children of light, disciples reflect God's character to such an extent that people see what God is like when they meet His disciples.

Finally, *disciples live in wisdom.* They skillfully apply God's principles in daily life. They don't just have knowledge; they know how to use it. The essence of the Christian life is to bring Christ to bear on how we live. It isn't simply a life of "dos and don'ts"; it's a life that is qualitatively different. Such a life cannot help but make an impact on society.

When the church starts making disciples, we will see change in our society. The future of our nation depends on what the church does or does not do. When the people in the church start living as Christ's disciples, the world will take note. But if we who know God can't live right, then how can those who do not know God possibly live right? The church *must* make disciples. Then and only then will the church make the impact on society that God requires.

Jesus makes a wonderful promise to the church at the end of His vision statement in Matthew 28. He says He will be with us. If we are committed to being and making disciples, He will be with us *always.* He will not empower us when we're trying to do our own thing. But if we're going out into the world to make disciples, He is with us.

As we saw in chapter 4, Lot made a critical mistake. His faith was too personal. He didn't make disciples. He didn't go anywhere, baptize anyone, or teach anything. His faith fed only himself. He probably had a great personal devotional life, but he had no societal impact. As a result, there was no redemption for the society in which he lived. It was destroyed.

Our society, like Lot's, is headed for devastation. The only way to avoid destruction is through a right relationship with Christ. The only way people's lives and communities will change for the better is through a right relationship with Christ. But that relationship with Christ must first be lived out in the life of believers, individually and corporately. When that happens, the people in our society will see Christ because His disciples model the kingdom of God in every word and action. Then there will be hope for our society.

# 11

# The Ministries of the Church

Society at large does not take the church seriously, and it's not entirely society's fault. Why should the world take us seriously when we don't take ourselves or our Lord's commission to make disciples seriously? We have made it easy for the world to ignore us because we are not turning out disciples as Jesus commanded. Instead, we are turning out church members, and sometimes not even doing a good job of that. To impact society, many of our churches must go back to the drawing board. We must study Jesus' teaching on the ministry of the church and restructure ourselves to produce the kinds of Christians who can make a difference in the world.

After Jesus' resurrection, the disciples knew without a doubt that He was the Messiah. They had watched Him face rejection from the Jews and die on the cross. They had seen the empty tomb and saw Him alive again. They knew Him as their resurrected Lord. They knew that Jesus was who He said He was—the one who would bring God's kingdom to earth.

After all they had seen, they were excited about what Jesus would do next. They were particularly excited about the promised restoration of the kingdom of Israel. So they asked Him what the future held:

> And so when they had come together, they were asking Him, saying, "Lord, is it at this time You are restoring the kingdom to Israel?"
> He said to them, "It is not for you to know times or epochs which the Father has fixed by His own authority; but you shall receive power when the Holy Spirit has come upon you; and you shall be My witnesses both in

Jerusalem, and in all Judea and Samaria, and even to the remotest part of the earth." (Acts 1:6-8)

You can be sure that Jesus' answer surprised the disciples. He basically said, "Don't worry about that. It's none of your business. God will take care of it in His own time. But there is something else I want you to worry about, so listen carefully! You need to concern yourselves with how you're going to be My witnesses in this world until the Father brings His kingdom."

Consider for a moment the difference between what the disciples were thinking and what Jesus was thinking. The disciples understood who Jesus was and that when God's kingdom came to earth the world's power structure would change. They also knew that God would give them power in His kingdom. So they were looking forward to the time when, no longer the underdogs, they would rule with Jesus. They didn't understand the dynamic tension between waiting for and working for the kingdom.

Like many Christians today, the disciples had a faulty view of the future. They focused on Christ's future kingdom rather than on their responsibility to occupy enemy territory and represent His kingdom until He returns (Luke 19:13). The church's responsibility to occupy the world can by compared to what happened in 1983 on the island of Grenada. Due to the rise of Communist insurgency, the U.S. President ordered troops into Grenada. In just eight hours, the battle was over. However, many of the Communists would not accept defeat. Rather than surrender, they sniped at our troops from behind cars, buildings, and trees. So our troops remained there until the victory was secured and a new government was installed.

When Jesus died on the cross and rose from the dead, He was victorious over all God's enemies. He clearly won the victory. However, Satan and his followers have not accepted defeat and still try to claim victory. Thus, the victorious Christ has established His troops—the church—to secure the victory until He returns to set up His new government. The church is God's occupational force until He comes again. Rather than focusing on their future rule with Him, therefore, Jesus wanted the disciples to focus on their impact in the world and be ready to receive God's power through the Holy Spirit.

When God's people commit to being His disciples—to live under His authority in every aspect of life—the Holy Spirit empowers them to be God's witnesses. We don't receive power because we participate in good church programs or give money to the church or belong to a big, beautiful church. We receive power because the Holy Spirit becomes active in our lives. The power of the Holy Spirit enables us to implement God's Word in our lives, to be His disciples through our witness in the world.

In Acts 1:8 Jesus doesn't say His disciples will receive power to *do* witnessing; He says they will receive power to *be* witnesses. When the Holy Spirit empowers the church, God's people become His witnesses to the world outside the church. We become His witnesses by word and deed, by what we say and by how we live. We simply can't help being God's living testimony.

So the discipleship process by which God's people become God's witnesses is a vital part of the church's ministry. As we discovered in the previous chapter, God has commissioned the church to develop His people into disciples. Disciples are those people who have progressed from spiritual infancy to spiritual maturity. Spiritually mature Christians respond biblically to the issues of life. They live life from a divine frame of reference and thereby show the world what God is like.

Participation in the local church should be a life-giving experience that encourages and enables those who desire to be Christ's disciples to move toward spiritual maturity. Therefore, the various ministry programs of the church ought to support the making of disciples. Four church ministries are essential to fulfilling the purpose of revealing Jesus to the world: education, fellowship, worship, and outreach.

## DISCIPLES NEED KNOWLEDGE

I find it disturbing that so many Christians pride themselves on being spiritually ignorant. Some children know more Bible than their parents. If we are to bring God's agenda to bear on every aspect of life, we must know His Word and its application to every aspect of life. In God's eyes, there is no premium on spiritual ignorance. Spiritual knowledge is of vital importance in the life of the believer:

> For though we walk in the flesh, we do not war according to the flesh, for *the weapons of our warfare are not of the flesh, but divinely powerful for the destruction of fortresses.*
>
> *We are destroying speculations and every lofty thing raised up against the knowledge of God,* and we are taking every thought captive to the obedience of Christ. (2 Corinthians 10:3-5; italics added)

God has given us spiritual weapons—tools to tear down fortresses. It takes power to tear down fortresses. Yet God's people have the power to tear them down. We tear down fortresses by tearing down "every lofty thing raised up against the knowledge of God." God's people need knowledge to tear down the fortresses of crime, abortion, incest, divorce, poverty, pornography, and drugs.

Tearing down fortresses is not a passive pastime. The church is not a passive institution. Christians ought not to be passive. We must aggressively tear down the fortresses that stand against God. We aren't supposed to happily coexist with the fortresses. It isn't a matter of "live and let live." We are to destroy everything that stands against the knowledge of God. God is interested not only in knowledge but in the action that knowledge inspires.

God wants His disciples to have knowledge to live transformed lives. He is interested in comprehensive Christianity. He is interested in a Christianity through which He can touch every aspect of life—finances, career, education, family, housing, recreation, clothing, personal relationships. He is interested in a Christianity in which everything we think about, say, or do comes under Jesus' authority. When we approach everything according to the will and Word of God, we will live transformed lives.

However, for Christ to influence everything in life, we need two kinds of knowledge. We need to know our Bible so that we know what He says, and we have to know how to apply that knowledge according to His authority. One way we gain knowledge is through expository preaching (see chapter 10). We also gain knowledge through personal study and meditation on God's Word.

Discipleship requires an ongoing, vital experience with God's Word. Jesus says this in John 8:31: "If you abide in My word, then you are truly disciples of Mine." Abiding in the Word enables us to become disciples. Abiding in the Word doesn't mean we listen to a sermon once in a while. It doesn't mean we read Scripture when we feel like it. Abiding in the Word means we have a dynamic relationship with the Word of God.

Many of us think that what we call "having devotions" is the same as abiding in the Word of God. It isn't. For many of us, devotions are a waste of time. Abiding in the Word of God isn't sitting down and picking out "a verse a day to keep the devil away." It isn't reading a verse and praying for God to use it in our life. It isn't casually opening the Bible and looking for a verse for the day. That's not developing a relationship with the Word of God.

Developing a relationship with God's Word that leads to spiritual knowledge means submitting our minds to God and discovering what all of Scripture says about the issues we face. It means getting out a concordance and studying related passages. It means gaining further understanding through a Bible commentary. It means talking with God about what's in

His Word and how it applies to our situation. It means expressing our desire to please Him in all aspects of life. It means learning how to apply God's Word to life.

That's the kind of biblical knowledge that disciples need to live transformed lives. That's the kind of biblical knowledge that the educational ministry of the church ought to encourage among God's people.

### DISCIPLES NEED FELLOWSHIP

If we are out in the world every day, seeking to live out God's agenda according to His authority, we're going to get beat up or worn out from time to time. So we need a place where we can take our bruised and beaten spirits and be lovingly ministered to by our brothers and sisters in Christ. We need a dynamic relationship with God's people. We need fellowship.

By fellowship, the Bible doesn't mean punch and cookies in the fellowship hall. Punch and cookies are pleasant, but they are no substitute for biblical fellowship. Biblical fellowship occurs when the people of God gather around the person of God to provide mutual encouragement in pursuing God's agenda. Fellowship means we encourage one another toward love and good deeds; we encourage each other to keep on keeping on (Hebrews 10:23-25).

Biblical fellowship—mutual encouragement and love for one another—is one of the key identifying marks of Christ's disciples. In John 13:34-35, Jesus gives His disciples what He calls a new commandment: "That you love one another, even as I have loved you, that you also love one another. By this all men will know that you are My disciples, if you have love for one another."

Our love for one another is to be as great as Jesus' love for us. Our love is supposed to be so deep—we are to be so tight—that we would die for one another. That's as deep as love gets. Most of us have that kind of love for our family members, but how many of us have that kind of love for our brothers and sisters in Christ?

Most of us won't lay down our lives for a stranger. So if we're going to lay down our lives for one another, we have to know each other. When we come together in fellowship to support one another in pursuing God's agenda, we get to know each other, care for each other, and learn to love each other as Christ commanded us. Thus, fellowship includes mutual ministry together.

Yes, fellowship can take place in a social setting, whether it be over a cup of coffee or dinner, but a social gathering doesn't automatically lead to fellowship. For instance, if you invite me over to your home to watch the football game, we may have a great time talking, laughing, and cheering our favorite team, but we haven't necessarily had Christian fellowship. Fellowship doesn't occur if the name of Jesus never comes up. We don't have fellowship if our purpose for meeting is anything other than building one another up to carry out God's agenda. That's the kind of fellowship the church must promote among its members.

### DISCIPLES NEED WORSHIP

To be Christ's disciples, we must have a vital relationship with God's person, which comes from worship. Worship is more than thinking about God and feeling a sense of awe. Worship brings us near to God. It is part of the process of finding out who we are and what we are supposed to do. Worship reminds us that Jesus' death on the cross is the center and starting point of our new life in Him. Worship is an essential part of the disciple's life. Worship is submitting all that we are to all that He is.

Acts 2:42-43 describes how the disciples worshiped together: "And they were continually devoting themselves to the apostles' teaching and to fellowship, to the breaking of bread and to prayer. And everyone kept feeling a sense of awe." Notice that the worship was the breaking of the bread—Communion—and prayer. The disciples broke bread together continually as a constant reminder that life begins at Calvary.

God's people today need to do the same thing. When we hit Monday morning, it's easy to forget our center point. So Communion is not a boring, repetitive exercise. By sharing Communion, we reestablish our theological frame of reference; we reestablish Christ as our center point. Any Christian who doesn't regularly come back to Calvary is a Christian without a center point.

After they celebrated Communion together, the Christians of Acts devoted themselves to prayer. Prayer, like Communion, is a form of worship. It is part of having a vital relationship with God. As we saw in 2 Corinthians 10:5, living under Christ's authority means that we take every thought captive to the mind of Christ. When we pray, that happens; Jesus takes our minds captive. If He is taking our minds captive, prayer is no longer a boring exercise. When Jesus takes our minds captive, we have plenty to pray about—we want to talk to Jesus about every part of life, because every part of life is related to Him.

Unfortunately, prayer is often the last thing we do. We usually pray only after all else fails. But that's not what God intends. In fact, if we can't pray for an hour, Jesus says we're not serious about prayer (Matthew 26:40-41). We can do many things for an hour. We can watch television for an hour. That's easy. We can talk on the phone for an hour. No problem. We can exercise for an hour. (Well, some of us can.) It's easy to do these activities for an hour or more because we derive enjoyment or other benefit from doing them. When Jesus is our center point, when we give every thought to Him, we will want to pray because we will want to have His viewpoint on everything.

Notice the result that worship produced in the lives of the disciples of Acts: "Everyone kept feeling a sense of awe." That's nice. We like to feel good. In fact, some of us don't understand the relationship of worship to good feelings. Some of us think that if we don't have the good feelings, we can't worship. That's not how worship works. God's people feel good as a *result* of worship, not as a *prerequisite* to worship.

It's possible to have good feelings that are totally wrong. For instance, you can get a good feeling from drugs, but it's from the wrong source. Our feelings must be based on fact because then we not only feel good, but we feel good for the right reasons.

Many Christians aren't on the cutting edge of representing Christ because they are trying to feel good without the worship. But when we worship first, when we reestablish Christ as the center point of our lives, the feelings will come. We will have a vital relationship with God's person that will fill us with awe.

### DISCIPLES NEED OUTREACH

The power of the Holy Spirit propels the church to go beyond its four walls and into the world. The Holy Spirit gives the church the power to be what God has called it to be—the visible demonstration of Jesus Christ in the world. It enables the church to minister *to the world*. Our ministry is to let the world know who Jesus is. If the world doesn't know Jesus, then we have failed.

As God's people, we need an ongoing experience with God's purpose for us. We need firsthand experience in being His witnesses. Jesus said, "By this is My Father glorified, that you bear much fruit, and so prove to be My disciples" (John 15:8). Bearing fruit is an essential part of the disciple's life. The fruit of our lives proves our commitment to Jesus. We can't say we are Christ's disciples if we are not touching someone else's life with the message of Christ. So outreach enables us to have a dynamic relationship with God's purpose.

A church that has its ministries of education, fellowship, worship, and outreach in order will be successful in making disciples. Such a church has a powerful ministry that can't help but overflow into the world. Such a church becomes the royal priesthood God intends it to be—the powerful, righteous entity that makes an impact on society. Such a church helps God's people bring every part of life into proper relationship with Him so that His image will go out into the world.

Acts 2:47 shows what happens when the church ministers appropriately to God's people: "And the Lord was adding to their number day by day those who were being saved." Everybody was talking about the church in Jerusalem. People were being saved—not just once in a while, but every day. Needs were being met, and the world noticed (Acts 2:47).

People were saved through the ministry of God's people because His church ministered fully. The church had an education program that helped the people learn what they needed to know and encouraged them to apply it by bringing every thought captive to Christ. It had a dynamic fellowship that centered on Christ. It had a dynamic worship that served as a non-stop reminder of Calvary. And it had a dynamic outreach empowered by the Holy Spirit. As a result, the people were enabled to become disciples who could impact their world.

# Part 3

# The Program

# 12

## The Church and Social Action

We live in a depraved world. We live in a world that has cut itself off from God and is reaping the disastrous results. Our world desperately needs the church to brilliantly reflect the spiritual and social environment God desires for all mankind.

In earlier chapters, we explored the foundation upon which the church can develop an appropriate social ministry to the world. We studied the basic spiritual conflict between God and Satan that underlies every problem and need in society. We defined the purpose and ministry of the church as God intended. We examined the shortcomings of the church and what the church must do to correct itself. We can now address the question, "How can the church make an impact on our society?"

Until we as God's people know who we are to be and who we represent, the church cannot have an effective ministry to the world. Until the church is what it is supposed to be, it has nothing to offer the world. Therefore, it is imperative that we live in such a way that we reveal the image of God in every part of life. The church can minister through social action when and only when it is the redemptive entity God has called it to be.

The social responsibility of the church is to execute divine justice on behalf of the defenseless people in society. The church accomplishes social action in relation to a just God, as a natural reflection of His glory. Furthermore, Christian social action begins in the church community, with the members of God's family, and then overflows into society. Christian social action, then, is a result of God's people becoming what God has called them to be and fulfilling what He has called them to do.

Although it is a result of the life of the church, social action isn't optional, it is an integral part of church ministry. Today there is a great deal of confusion about whether social outreach is part of the gospel or simply a distinct application of the gospel. Some Christians believe that to *include* social ministry in the gospel is to preach a "different gospel." Others believe that to *exclude* social ministry as part of the gospel message is to deny the gospel. In fact, a sociological, political, and theological movement called Liberation Theology has been formed upon this latter thesis.

To resolve the conflict, we must make a distinction between the gospel's content and its scope. The content of the gospel message is limited. Paul makes this unmistakably clear in his declaration that Jesus' death and resurrection and our personal response to His redemptive work is the only message of the gospel (1 Corinthians 15:1-4). On the other hand, social action is a legitimate part of the gospel's scope. Paul uses the word *gospel* not only to describe how a person develops a relationship with God, but to describe the social impact of a Christian's life. For example, Paul tells the Christians in Rome that the gospel establishes them (Romans 16:25). He also tells the Corinthians that they fulfill the ministry of the gospel by meeting the financial needs of their fellow Christians (2 Corinthians 9:12-13).

Therefore, the church is to deliver the content of the gospel so that people come into a personal relationship with God. Also, we are to live out the scope of the gospel so that people can see our good deeds and glorify God. Since the purpose of Christian social action is to reflect God's justice to the world, social ministry is vitally linked to the overall purpose of the church, although it does not constitute the means of personal forgiveness.

## THE OLD TESTAMENT BASIS FOR SOCIAL ACTION

God is just. He desires deliverance from oppression for all people. Because He is just, He desires that justice prevail in the world. The Old Testament portrays God as the prime example of social justice in action. Repeatedly God demonstrates Himself as a deliverer. Time and time again, He provides justice and freedom from oppression—especially for His people.

The Exodus event, for instance, is a dramatic example of God's executing social action on behalf of the nation Israel. The Israelites were oppressed—politically, spiritually, and socially. God, through His servant Moses, directly intervened to deliver them from their Egyptian oppressors.

Later, when God dictated His laws to Israel, He said, "You shall not wrong a stranger or oppress him, for you were strangers in the land of Egypt" (Exodus 22:21). God reminded the Israelites of their former oppression. He made clear that, because He had delivered them from oppression, He wanted them to have no part in oppressing others. It is human nature for those who have been oppressed, and then rise to a position of power, to become just like their former oppressors. But that is not how God wants His people to treat others. He is a God of justice, and He wants us to imitate His justice in every area of life.

God also provided deliverance from oppression through the year of Jubilee, which is presented in Leviticus 25. Every fiftieth year, God ordained that slaves be set free, debts canceled, and real property revert back to its original owners. The year of Jubilee renewed freedom for people at all levels of life. It reflected the justice and righteousness God intends for all mankind to enjoy.

However, there was more to the year of Jubilee than just freedom. The year of Jubilee accompanied the Day of Atonement, during which time the people repented from their sins and reestablished a right relationship with God. So Jubilee was a direct result of atonement. The people enjoyed God's freedom in society because they were righteous before Him.

As we consider social ministry today, we must not forget that freedom and justice are the results of righteousness before God. Our society ignores the fact that ultimate freedom exists only as a result of right relationship with God. Without that relationship, there is no guarantee of freedom.

For example, the black community in the sixties made great strides toward freedom from oppression. Led by the church, that movement had tremendous social impact. But twenty-five years later, some things are better, but the overall plight of a large group of black Americans is worse than before.

The question we have to ask is, "How could that have happened? How could so much progress be reversed?" Righteous principles can temporarily impact society, but unless righteous people step in to guarantee that impact at all levels of society it will not last. Secular society can't guarantee freedom. It can't even guarantee that it will abide by its own rules.

All people need a place where they know they will be free. They need a place where they know they will be treated with respect. They need a place where they know they will be loved. The only place that can guarantee such deliverance is the place where the people are right with God. God has always desired such a place for mankind. In the Old Testament, that place was the nation Israel. In the New Testament, that place was the church. Today, that place is still the church.

We must never forget that there is a connection between knowing God and knowing justice. Although the theme of God's justice and deliverance is illustrated throughout all of Scripture, the Old Testament prophets provide the greatest information on social action. The prophets presented God's viewpoint on social justice. They repeatedly tied oppression directly to society's spiritual departure from God.

For example, Israel's worship was rejected because of an absence of justice in society (Amos 5:21-24). The Israelites were taken into captivity and held in bondage because of their rebellion against God (Ezekiel 33:10-33). In Malachi 3:5, God personally promises to judge those who oppress others. And God promises blessing to Israel only if it practices justice (Zechariah 8:14-17).

Our God delights in justice and righteousness. Jeremiah 9:24 says, "But let him who boasts boast of this, that he understands and knows Me, that I am the Lord who exercises lovingkindness, justice, and righteousness on earth; for I delight in these things." If we say we know God, then we ought to know justice. God, justice, and righteousness always go together. Thus, as God's righteous people, we are necessary in providing deliverance from oppression at all levels of society.

## JESUS: SOCIAL ACTION IN PERSPECTIVE

In the New Testament, we continue to see God as the deliverer of His people. This time, deliverance was provided through the God-man, Jesus. Jesus fully understood the nature of His ministry and its potential for social impact. His perspective on social ministry is helpful for the church today.

Jesus often taught in the synagogue. One day He read these words from the book of Isaiah:

> The Spirit of the Lord is upon Me,
> Because He anointed Me to preach the gospel to the poor.
> He has sent Me to proclaim release to the captives,
> And recovery of sight to the blind,
> To set free those who are downtrodden,
> To proclaim the favorable year of the Lord.
> (Luke 4:18)

After reading this prophecy, Jesus said, "Today this Scripture has been fulfilled in your hearing" (Luke 4:21).

Jesus was saying that He was the one to proclaim deliverance. He was the one to atone for man's sin and pave the way for the eternal year of

Jubilee. Jesus proclaimed freedom to the captives but didn't say He would set them free. What's the difference between *proclaiming* freedom and *giving* freedom? Jesus proclaimed the good news that will set men free, but He didn't automatically set us free. The guarantee of our freedom depends on our response to His atonement.

Jubilee is the result of atonement. Jesus couldn't give Jubilee to the Jews because they refused to deal with their sin. They refused to be made right with God. Jesus would have provided them with the deliverance from Rome they so much desired, if they had atoned for their sins. However, the Jews wanted the benefits of the Messiah without the relationship with the Messiah. They wanted Jubilee without atonement. That's not how God's justice works. No guarantee of deliverance exists without atonement.

Jesus' ministry gives us a proper perspective on how to approach our ministry to social needs. He could have snapped His fingers and delivered all the poor, the widows, and the oppressed. However, Jesus was very particular about His social involvement. He became involved when He could also proclaim His message. His purpose was to preach and teach the kingdom of God. So He preached; as He preached He came across needs that He met.

Jesus didn't stop preaching to meet social needs. He knew His purpose was to build God's kingdom, not just meet social needs. All the social activity the world can muster will not solve the world's problems. In the long term, social action is limited; lasting solutions can only come from the kingdom of God because that's where the atonement that guarantees deliverance occurs.

Jesus' feeding of the 5,000 (John 6:1-15) illustrates His approach to social ministry. While preaching, Jesus recognized that the people needed food. Only a few loaves of bread and a couple of fish were available—not much more than sardines and crackers to us. Yet when Jesus blessed that food, it became enough to feed everyone—men, women, and children. It was like an all-you-can-eat buffet. After everyone had eaten "his fill," Jesus' disciples gathered up a dozen baskets of leftovers.

The people Jesus fed weren't dumb. They saw Jesus as a fantastic welfare program. They wanted to make the man who could pray over sardines and crackers and turn them into "Moby Dick" sandwiches their king. How did Jesus respond? He went away. He wasn't on earth to be a welfare king; He was on earth to be King of kings and Lord of lords. Nothing could deter Him from His real purpose.

The church needs to adopt Jesus' perspective. We aren't trying to save the world's system. It's going downhill fast. However, we are trying to reveal a different system, one created by God, that provides a divine alternative so that the world can see what God's system is like. We are trying to show God's glory in every area of life, including the meeting of social needs. By doing so, we help others see the reality of Christ. Our overriding goal is disciplemaking, and social ministry is a good way to reach those who would become Christ's disciples.

One reason the church has often failed in having both an effective social impact and an evangelistic outreach is because it has joined with the world's social agenda rather than adhering to God's agenda. Biblical social action may not at first receive its rightful recognition, but it is the only way to make a real difference in society. When the secular world sees that the church has indeed built a better mousetrap, it will waste no time in emulating it.

### THE CHURCH'S SOCIAL MINISTRY IN PERSPECTIVE

One of the premier roles of the church is to *model* divine righteousness to the world. Christians can't just tell secular society what to do; they have to be living examples of what to do. That is what the Holy Spirit has empowered the church to accomplish.

The church cannot expect society—which doesn't have the power—to do what only the church has the power to do (but doesn't do). Therefore, it is essential that we *proclaim* as well as *model* social action. The church has often erred in its approach to social ministry. Two main flaws have been evident.

First, the church sometimes attempts to solve problems in the community that have not been resolved in the church. If the problems of a few hundred people in the church can't be solved, how can we possibly solve the problems facing a community of thousands? Why should the community accept "solutions" that haven't been tried or perhaps have even failed in the church?

If a man wants to be an elder but has not demonstrated proper leadership in his home, 1 Timothy 3:4-5 says that he is not qualified for the position. By the same principle, a church that doesn't feed its hungry, support its widows, provide jobs for its unemployed, discipline its rebellious members, and provide homes for its fatherless is unqualified to lead the world in making a social impact. We cannot expect society to believe that we have solutions to more widespread and complex problems if we can't solve those problems in our own house.

In fact, at times secular society (perhaps unknowingly) successfully uses biblical principles. Some non-Christian couples, for example, may have better marriages than some Christians because they more consistently apply the biblical principle of sacrificial love. Some children of non-Christians may be more disciplined than some children of Christians because their parents use the rod more consistently. And some non-Christian agencies may be more effective in meeting social needs than some churches because they more faithfully apply the principle of loving one's neighbor.

Second, the church has sometimes forgotten that its main purpose in ministry is to make disciples, not to solve every problem in society. The magnitude of society's problems are far greater than the local church can deal with effectively. People's needs are endless. There is no way the church can meet every need.

Jesus, who certainly had the ability to solve every problem and meet every need, had the wisdom to refuse to allow needs to dictate His actions. He fed the hungry, but He did not attempt to feed all of them. He healed the sick, but not all of them. He raised the dead, but not all of the dead. He understood that meeting needs was *part* of His ministry, not the *purpose* of it.

We too must remember that social action only assists us in achieving our greater goal. Making disciples is ultimately more important than feeding people. Disciples are made only through the ministry of other disciples. It is the proliferation of disciples that produces an atmosphere of righteousness in society. Recognizing this truth, we must also remember that discipleship without tangible social impact is faulty (James 1:27; 2:14-17).

Without an understanding of the relationship of discipleship and social action, the church allows the secular world to force its agenda upon it. However, the church is supposed to set the agenda. If secular society doesn't want our agenda, that is their loss. We dare not lessen our biblical perspective to accommodate the unrighteous.

## A PHILOSOPHY OF SOCIAL MINISTRY

What is the biblical way for the church to approach social ministry? The philosophy of social ministry is presented in Galatians 6:10: "Let us do good to all men, and especially to those who are of the household of the faith." God's people have a burden to minister to all people because all people bear the image of God, but we cannot start with a ministry to everyone. There is a "pecking order" to social action. Our ministry must begin in the community of people who belong to God. Therefore, social ministry begins when we start to alleviate suffering within the church.

We see evidence of such a philosophy of ministry in the book of Acts. What makes Acts dynamic is not that all the Roman Empire's problems were solved. The dynamic is that all the needs of the community of believers were met so that the ministry of the church overflowed and influenced the whole empire. The same principle ought to be true of the church's social ministry today.

The church's ministry is to be so powerful and effective within itself that it overflows into the community. The community thereby benefits from the residual effect of what is happening in the church. This principle was at work early in the development of our nation. Puritan Christianity provided an overflow of righteousness into the community. One result of that overflow was the structure of our government, which was established on the biblical principles of justice and freedom. Although those principles have not always been applied consistently or equally, they are basically biblical.

Furthermore, it is imperative that the church approach social ministry from a theological standpoint. As God's people, we are spiritual. Therefore, we understand the spiritual reality behind physical problems. By addressing the underlying theological or spiritual issues, we can achieve long-term solutions that solve physical problems because we have addressed the entire problem, not just its physical manifestation. Long-term, practical solutions are a result of good theology applied by the church.

Remember Jesus' response to Satan's temptation (chapter 7)? Satan presented Jesus with a physical need (hunger), but Jesus responded to the need in terms of theology. Jesus understood that man doesn't live by physical reality alone. Because man lives through the dynamic interplay of the spiritual and the physical, Jesus used the written Word to address a physical need. He made sure He had His theology right before He attempted to meet His physical need. Likewise, social ministry in the church must first encompass the spiritual and then the physical.

To arrive at a biblical action plan, we should do what Jesus did when He confronted Satan's agenda. That is, we look to the Old Testament to discover what social solutions God provided for His people. We then apply those solutions to contemporary problems within the context and framework of New Testament instructions.

The New Testament rarely addresses specific social programs because the answers were already provided through God's interaction with man in the Old Testament. This is why the New Testament authors often quoted the Old Testament in their writings. First Corinthians 10:6, for instance, shows that Paul understood that the Old Testament offered behavioral examples for Christians.

When applying Old Testament examples, however, we must ensure that they do not negate or supersede New Testament theology. For example, if we want to address the problem of crime, we must discover what was practiced in the Old Testament and ensure that it does not contradict the New Testament principle. If the practice and principle are compatible, we can duplicate the practice in contemporary society. With regard to crime, there are two biblical options: restitution or death. There is no biblical provision for prisons. This process can be applied to every social issue we face.

What this means to our society is that nobody can address social problems like the church can. The church has a handle on the hidden ingredient—theology—that makes long-term solutions to society's problems possible. Secular society does not understand the spiritual reality that causes physical problems. So society only has physical ingredients to work with, and that isn't enough.

### THE CHURCH AS THE IDEAL
### FACILITATOR OF SOCIAL ACTION

Because of its spiritual perspective and power, the church is the ideal entity for meeting the needs of our society. The church is ideal for pragmatic reasons as well. It has the physical resources—the people and facilities—necessary to carry out social action.

For example, churches offer the largest, most qualified volunteer force in the nation. No group can compare with the church in terms of numbers of people available to attack the problems of our day. Of course, it will take some work to get God's people out of the pew and into the action, but once that is achieved there will be no lack of people to accomplish the task of biblically based social revitalization.

Churches also provide a setting for accountability. Few social agencies gather their people together for renewal and training every week, but the church does. When people are confronted with their spiritual agenda every week, it remains a high priority. In addition, the authority structure of the church can hold people accountable to accomplish the work of social ministry.

Since churches exist in every community, the structure to address social problems already exists. We don't have to create new institutions to implement solutions because the church is already within reach of every needy person. The church is ideally suited to serve as a rallying force in the community. Churches can help recapture a sense of community spirit from which community social action can result. In addition, churches have existing facilities to house social programs. When these facilities are fully utilized, there will be little need to build new social service facilities.

### SOCIETY NEEDS THE SOCIAL MINISTRY OF THE CHURCH

The social ministry of the church is necessary to the redemption of society. We have already established that the fundamental cause of our society's decline is the loss of a moral frame of reference. Our world is in the shape it's in because people have rejected the God of freedom and deliverance. They want deliverance, but they don't want the Lord who delivers. Like the Jews of Jesus' day, our society wants Jubilee without atonement. That is impossible.

Our world needs atonement. It needs to rebuild itself on moral values. The church is the only entity that can bring about such change because it is made up of righteous people whose sins have been forgiven. Therefore, the church is made up of people who can demonstrate what divine social action is supposed to look like.

The job of the church is to proclaim, model, and transfer God's system of moral values to every corner of the world. Since the church functions by God's absolute standards, which apply to every area of life, it can lead the way in solving our fundamental problem of moral collapse. The church can guarantee Jubilee because its people are right with God.

Society has tried—through people, movements, money, programs—to save itself. Yet it continues to decline at an ever-increasing rate. Despite grandiose efforts, Humpty Dumpty still lies shattered on the ground. The only way to make Humpty Dumpty whole again is through the church. The only way to make our communities whole again is through the church. The only way to heal our cities is through the church.

For these reasons, the church must fight to keep God at the center of society, while also maintaining the institutional separation of church and state. When God is dismissed from society, so are morality, decency, values, family stability, and meaning in life. Therefore, we cannot allow the government, media, courts, or educational system to push us into a small corner of society. Theologically and practically, the church is the world's best and only hope. We must not allow the world to dismiss us so easily.

Yes, the solution to society's woes already exists in the church. God's people have been given the vision, the resources, and the responsibility to model God's kingdom on earth. It is time for the church to pursue its mission of making disciples, thereby becoming a powerful agent for social change. The church doesn't need to abandon God's agenda by adopting secular strategies for social action. When the church is fulfilling God's agenda in every area of life, its social ministry will be so powerful that it will overflow into the secular community.

People in the secular world may not like Christ, but they like the church when it has real solutions to seemingly insurmountable problems. The secular world is beginning to realize that it doesn't know what to do about society's problems. So it notices Christian social action that works.

# 13

# The Church and Charity

Recently a fire completely destroyed the home of one of the members of our church in Dallas. The family lost everything. However, within twenty-four hours they had been housed, clothed, and fed. They had also received donated furniture and money to help them reestablish their home life.

These needs were met through the care-cell system of our church. We have a 2,000-member church which is organized into small groups of twenty-five families we call care cells. These minichurch units are designed to provide a relational context of care and support among our members. In difficult circumstances like those described above, such caring relationships are essential.

This testimony of love shown by God's people truly reveals God's love to the broader community. But as in all social involvement, the church must follow biblical guidelines in helping those who are needy. People with a deep desire to see human suffering alleviated in society have formed whole movements to combat the problem yet have often started from the wrong premise. The church cannot afford to respond in charity on a purely emotional level. We must operate according to God's agenda, as presented in Scripture.

The Bible offers a generic guideline for our response to human needs: if we see a brother in need and have the resources to meet that need, then that person is our neighbor whom we should care for (Luke 10:29-37). By this definition, we have neighbors all over the world. People who are starving in Ethiopia are just as much our neighbors as people in our country who are losing their farms and people down the street who are unemployed.

The Bible gives clear priorities for meeting social needs. In 1 Timothy 5:8 we learn that our first responsibility is to see that members of our immediate family have all the basic necessities—that they have food, clothing, and a place to sleep. When those needs have been met, Galatians 6:10 says that we are responsible for what the Bible calls the household of faith—our brothers and sisters in Christ who are part of our immediate fellowship, as well as those in other local churches. We are to guarantee that the life-supporting needs of our physical and spiritual families are met. Beyond those responsibilities, we are to respond to the community at large as we are able.

## UNITY ENABLES THE CHURCH
## TO CARE ENOUGH TO SHARE

The early church, as it is portrayed in the book of Acts, beautifully illustrates the practical side of biblical ministry to the poor. In Acts 4:32, we see a dynamic, developing, and unified church: "The congregation of those who believed were of one heart and soul." A spirit of harmony prevailed. The people had not only accepted Jesus as Savior but had taken Him seriously as Lord. They had gathered around Jesus and pursued a unified mission to make Him known throughout the Roman Empire. They were united by a commitment to live in such a way that the world would see their love for God and for each other.

We've recently seen what happens in secular society when people are unified. The changes in Eastern Europe during the last quarter of 1989 are a dramatic example of unity at work. The turnstiles of freedom are moving because the people have risen up with one voice.

Now just imagine what God's people today could do—what changes we could bring about—if we were unified. What would the church be like if we were "of one heart and soul"? We need only look at the early church to find out.

Luke describes the results of unity in the church in Acts 4:33: "And with great power the apostles were giving witness to the resurrection of the Lord Jesus, and abundant grace was upon them all." The apostles had great power in proclaiming the Word because the congregation was unified. Unity led to a powerful ministry, and also led to abundant grace—provision from heaven.

Notice how this unity demonstrated itself: "And not one of them claimed that anything belonging to him was his own; but all things were common property to them" (Acts 4:32). The unity of the early believers was so strong that they even overcame their natural selfishness. They began caring deeply for one another and sharing everything.

Today we live in a selfish world, a world that has little sharing or caring left. In our world, life is cheap. If we make someone angry on the highway, we could be killed. There are few safe, caring places left in our world. With four thousand fetuses being destroyed every day, even the womb isn't a safe place to be. In a world like this, people need to see an oasis of care. They need a place where they can know that somebody cares enough to share. The church can and ought to be such a place.

The early church gives us a real-life example of how we should care for one another by sharing. Even though people in the church were free to manage their own possessions, Acts 4:32 makes clear that everyone in the community enjoyed the benefit of those possessions. This is very difficult for Christians today to understand. We read that "all things were common property" and imagine utter chaos. We imagine others coming into our homes at any time and taking anything they want. But that's not the case at all. The issue here is what the believers *claimed*, not what they had.

Acts 4:32 doesn't say that nothing belonged to anyone; it says that no person claimed any belongings. Their possessions were theirs, but they didn't hold their possessions selfishly. They had such strong unity that they allowed their material possessions to be used for the good of the body. Sharing wasn't a problem.

Such sharing has existed in other church communities in the past. For instance, the black church in America has demonstrated this kind of love for one another. This love was particularly evident during the years 1787 through 1865, when the black community suffered in slavery. At a time when black people had almost nothing in the way of material resources or possessions, the black church managed to take care of its own. In fact, the enslaved black church is probably the greatest community-wide expression of biblical Christianity in the history of this country.

The reason this idea of sharing is so difficult for us today is not because we have possessions but that we grasp them tightly—we lay claim to them. In other words, we exercise exclusive rights over the resources God has given us to manage. Instead of sharing our resources for the good of the body, we seldom make what we have available to the church.

We generally do not think biblically when it comes to caring and sharing. We don't want the burden of caring; we only want to receive the blessings of the ministry. So if we make more money, we live better. We use the additional money for greater personal enjoyment, or we use it to make more money. While this is not necessarily wrong, we must also use our resources to promote the kingdom of God.

We need to have a renewed vision for sharing and meeting one another's needs in the church. Sharing in the church is a bit like the sharing that takes place in marriage. When we marry, we turn what's "mine" into what's "ours." Our failure to have such an attitude of sharing in the church prohibits us from being a family.

Part of being in God's family is learning how to share with one another, for we are merely stewards of what God has given us. Nothing belongs to us to the point that we are sovereign over it. We were born with nothing and will die the same way—naked and broke.

The members of the early church, however, understood stewardship and what it meant to share. They put their money where their mouth was: "There was not a needy person among them, for all who were owners of land or houses would sell them and bring the proceeds of the sales, and lay them at the apostles' feet, and they would be distributed to each, as any had need" (Acts 4:34-35). The early believers truly understood that they owned nothing but could use everything God gave them. So they willingly brought their money to the church to be used for God's glory.

## GOD TAKES SHARING SERIOUSLY

The Christians in the early church not only shared their possessions, they even liquidated assets to support God's family. But not everyone shared wholeheartedly. In Acts 5:1-11, we read about a couple who conspired to defraud the church and God.

The couple, named Ananias and Sapphira, sold a piece of land and said that they wanted to give the proceeds to the church. However, they secretly agreed to keep some of the money for themselves. They wanted to look spiritual—like they were helping the family of God—while making a profit.

However, God doesn't allow His people to mess around with Him. Through the Holy Spirit, Peter suspected that something was amiss. So he separately questioned Ananias and Sapphira about their gift. Each of them lied, saying they had given *all* the money from the sale of their land to the church, and both of them were struck dead immediately.

This illustration communicates important principles about the use of wealth in God's kingdom. First, we must realize that what we have belongs to God. Some of us are blessed with many things; others are blessed with fewer things. God doesn't ask us to give what we don't have, but He expects us to make a real commitment to Him. Second, once we make a commitment to Him, God takes it seriously. He holds us accountable to keep that commitment.

You see, the issue with Ananias and Sapphira wasn't the money; it was their commitment. The land was theirs. They were not obligated to sell it. They were not obligated to give the money to the church. However, they lied about their commitment to God. They played games with God. They made a promise to Him that they never intended to keep.

Many people today want to play games with God too. Some want the benefits of the church, but they don't want to make a serious commitment. They don't want to care enough to make their time, energy, and resources available for the kingdom. They don't want to help a brother who's down, or a sister who is hurting. All they want is a sermon and a song.

However, God calls us to a serious commitment—to be part of the family of God. In the same way a family unites to care for its members, we must care enough to share what God has given us. Caring in the church is more than shaking someone's hand and saying, "I love you." Caring is an investment of time, an investment of energy, an investment of resources.

## USING WEALTH FOR GOD'S PURPOSES

We might be tempted to overlook the fact that the church in Jerusalem included wealthy people, not just poor people. These wealthy people had investments, owned property, and had the resources to help meet the economic needs of the church. Because of their unified purpose and love for one another, they used their resources to build up the kingdom of God. It was unthinkable for them to expect anyone outside the family of God to care for their less fortunate members.

The same ought to true of the church today. God raises up people in His church who have the ability to earn money, manage resources, and make profitable investments. The income we earn, however, never stays neutral; it either goes to the devil or it goes to the Lord (Matthew 6:24). So we must have the theology to use our financial resources correctly—to benefit the kingdom of God (Luke 16:1-13).

There's nothing wrong with the ability to accumulate wealth. Those who are doing well financially, however, have a greater responsibility to share with those who have needs. The purpose of wealth is not just so we can have a bigger house, bigger cars, and designer clothes. Wealth enables us to promote and fund the kingdom of God—to meet needs.

In Acts people brought money to the church leaders so that it might be distributed "to anyone as he had need," according to biblical guidelines.

The church was the central distribution center for meeting the physical needs of the congregation.

This is an important principle to note. Some people will express a need to the church so they can rip it off. They'll tell ten different people that they need fifty dollars to buy groceries. If each of those people responds, they've got $500. So someone in the church needs to be responsible for verifying expressed needs. The people in the early church who requested money couldn't make up stories about needs because the church leaders ensured that the money would be used correctly.

An accountability system must be in place for the church to effectively meet financial needs. First of all, a need (such as for food, clothing, or shelter) must be established. Second, the distribution process should, more often than not, meet the need directly (i.e., by sending the check directly to the mortgage or utility company) rather than just handing out money. Third, designated leaders should handle this ministry so that people cannot obtain duplicate assistance from the church. To assure that the church is not contributing to an individual's irresponsibility, the church should provide training in the biblical concepts of financial management, especially budgeting. The church should also ensure that the person has a realistic budget. People who don't want this accountability don't really want the help.

Of course, the church should also have food pantries that provide immediate relief when needed. The legendary Dr. E. V. Hill of the Mt. Zion Missionary Baptist Church in Los Angeles has turned charity into a biblical art form. His famed Lord's Kitchen feeds hundreds of people each week, and his Fragment Center provides clothes for those who need them. Some churches I know of joined together to create a large food bank, which members of all participating churches can use. As long as a church provides volunteers to help staff the bank and supports the bank financially, it can participate. To use the food bank, a person seeking assistance must have a request form signed by a designated leader of his or her church. This assures that the user is in proper standing with the church. This process forces accountability of the user as well as the church and establishes the church as the primary channel through which needs are met.

In society, we usually try to meet needs by giving money, but that's often not the best way, nor the biblical way, to meet needs. The preferable way to meet needs in God's family is by providing employment for those who don't have the resources to live. The next chapter is devoted to the philosophy and suggested methods for providing employment through the church. However, certain classifications of people are not able to be employed, and therefore need a different kind of assistance. In the case of an older widow who has no children, for example, the church must provide for her needs (1 Timothy 5:1-16). These needs can be met through outright gifts, or—when appropriate—through loans.

The Bible generally discourages borrowing. Proverbs 22:7 says that a borrower becomes a slave to the lender. Heavy indebtedness is a consequence of ignoring God's statutes and commandments (Deuteronomy 28:15, 43-45). However, loans that help the poor in their time of need—to provide basics such as food, clothing, and shelter—are an appropriate way of caring for one another (Exodus 22:25-27). Such loans are to be interest free, because the purpose of the loan isn't to make money but to help a needy member of God's family (Exodus 22:25; Leviticus 25:35-37).

In the Bible, loans had to be limited to no more than seven years to protect the poor from entering into long-term liability. In addition, the lender could take collateral to inconvenience the borrower so that he would have incentive to repay the loan quickly (Exodus 22:26-27; Deuteronomy 24:12-13). A lender could take a man's coat—even his last coat to give the borrower an incentive to work. However, the lender had to return the borrower's coat at the end of the day so he wouldn't freeze to death at night. Sensitivity to the borrower's survival was balanced by an inconvenience that encouraged responsibility.

In keeping with this guideline, our church policy states that people who receive interest-free loans are to bring their cars to the church every morning and leave the keys. They have to find their own way to and from work, but at the end of the day they can pick up their cars. It's a great inconvenience to not have a car during the day, but the cars are not totally removed from them. This inconvenience also forces people to ask themselves whether they really need a loan.

There are other things the church and its members can do to show responsible charity. The church building, which often sits empty many nights of the week, could be used for emergency shelter for the homeless while they seek employment. Such shelter could be provided in exchange for a few hours of donated labor to the church. Families in the church could provide friendship to the homeless people and perhaps a home-cooked meal.

The Bible teaches that one of the marks of a dynamic church is the members' willingness to show hospitality to strangers (Hebrews 13:2; Romans 12:15). The biblical meaning of assisting strangers includes helping those who cannot help themselves (Matthew 20:35-37; Luke 10:25-37), as opposed to simply helping those who can return the favor next week. Homes can also be used to provide temporary assistance to those who are down and out until they are up and in.

My good friend Dr. Kenneth Ulmer, pastor of the Faithful Central Baptist Church in Los Angeles, has caught this vision for the homeless and is having immense success in implementing it. Two nights a week, his church is open to the homeless. Not only are they provided meals and a place to sleep, they are also given medical care, legal assistance, and other social service support. In fact, his members are now beginning to open their homes to provide on-going care for the homeless.

Confronting the issue of charity requires a unity within the church. When a collective group of believers come together to form one church, they are able to minister in effective, efficient, and spiritually empowered ways. It's not the work of a few professionals; it's the work of the whole body that rallies around instructions from Jesus Christ, our Lord.

# 14

# The Church and Poverty

Tom needed to develop a skill to increase his chances of finding meaningful employment. He enrolled in his church's data processing program. He learned computer skills, including the Lotus financial accounting system. Today he does accounting for a fast-food chain.

Gary is a businessman who lost his job when the economy turned downward. The church networked on his behalf with a local Christian businessman, and Gary became the first minority executive in the other Christian's company. The business owner remarked that the fact that the church stood behind Gary made all the difference in the world.

These are solutions to poverty and unemployment that work. One of the greatest flaws in society's efforts toward social revitalization is that the poor have been given more money and programs that have offered temporary financial relief but have enabled the poor simply to have more money with which to remain poor. The money and programs have done little to raise people from poverty to productivity. Little effort has been expended to develop skills or a productive mind-set. So when funding for programs ends, people dependent on those programs have been left with nothing. However, the Bible offers a different perspective and real solutions to the issues of poverty and productivity.

### BIBLICAL SOLUTIONS TO TWO KINDS OF POVERTY

As we consider how to meet the needs of the poor in society, we must remember that God is not on the side of all poor people just because they are poor. God recognizes that not everyone is poor for the same reasons. Apart from catastrophes that render people poor, the poor can be divided into two categories: those who are lazy, and those who are oppressed and therefore unable to improve their financial status.

God detests laziness. The Bible says that poor people who are lazy will not accomplish anything in life (Proverbs 15:19). It says they are victims of self-imposed bondage (Proverbs 12:24); they waste opportunities (Proverbs 6:9-10) and bring poverty on themselves (Proverbs 10:4). It also says that they are neglectful (Ecclesiastes 10:18) and unproductive (Matthew 25:26-30).

How should we respond to poverty that results from laziness? If people are poor because they are lazy, we have no responsibility to help them except to challenge them to be responsible. We are not to encourage irresponsibility. Proverbs repeatedly says that people who do not work should not expect to receive the resources necessary to sustain life (Proverbs 6:6-11; 13:4; 19:15). In 2 Thessalonians 3:10, Paul says, "If anyone will not work, neither let him eat!" People who expect others to do what God has given them the ability and responsibility to do for themselves should be given nothing—no deacons fund, no food pantry, no benefits.

If, on the other hand, people are poor because they are oppressed, then the church has a major responsibility. God is the ultimate deliverer of the oppressed (James 2:5; 5:1-8). Therefore, His church should lead the way in declaring the unrighteousness of oppression. His church should lead the way in actively resisting oppressors and should work diligently toward relief from all oppression.

Given these fundamental guidelines, the Bible's solution to poverty is productivity—or, to put it bluntly, work. The Bible says a lot about work. It says that work is holy (Ecclesiastes 2:24; 3:22) and is designed to benefit the worker (Proverbs 10:2-4; 12:1-12; 13:4, 11). It says that work enables the worker to provide for the family's physical welfare (1 Timothy 5:8). And, not surprisingly, it says that work benefits the church by furthering its ministry and making it possible to assist people who have needs (Ephesians 4:28).

The Old Testament concept of gleaning clearly illustrates the value of work and the kind of productivity that God expects of all people. Farmers and landowners in Old Testament times were instructed to leave the edges of their fields unharvested, and any poor people or foreigners who followed the harvesters were welcome to gather (glean) the grain that remained (Leviticus 19:9-10; 23:22; Deuteronomy 24:17-21). Gleaning, then, was the primary source of charity for the poor. It enabled the poor to work and provided them with the food they needed.

The question we need to address is how the church today can provide a contemporary equivalent of gleaning. I believe the church can do this by providing employment opportunities for the poor that enable them to work and become productive members of society. We can accomplish this not only by providing jobs but by offering training for underskilled workers.

## THE CHURCH CAN PROVIDE JOBS

No able-bodied member of the church ought to be dependent on welfare to live. The church is God's family, and the basic needs of all of its members ought to be met by the community of believers. One way the church can meet basic needs today is by helping its unemployed members find jobs. In fact, if the church is going to address the problem of poverty, it must get into the business of creating jobs. That's not as difficult as it sounds. A simple way to begin this process is through local church networking.

For example, if a suburban church becomes partners with an urban church, members of the suburban church who have jobs to offer can make those opportunities available to needy members of the urban church prior to advertising in the newspaper. Thus, employers have the opportunity to find employees and the unemployed have the opportunity to find a job.

An even greater benefit of church networking is that it allows the urban church to provide a solution to an urban problem while at the same time providing an accountability base for people who find jobs through the church. The employer can then have greater confidence in the hiring process because he or she knows that the church will hold those employees accountable. No classified ad section or secular employment agency can deliver this kind of accountability.

Furthermore, the networking process enables the church to take the lead in demonstrating how the private sector can begin to meet the needs of the unemployed. Rather than the church going to the government to ask for grants so it can carry on a job program, the church can meet those needs on its own.

Church networking isn't just a nice theory; it works. Such a program has been in effect in various churches around the country for some time. To start the process at our church, I called a Christian businessman in North Dallas and proposed a plan. "Instead of putting your job opportunities in the newspaper," I said, "would you call our church? We may already have someone trained for the position you need to fill. If not, perhaps we'd be able to train a person.

"I realize this is a new idea," I continued, "but as Christians, we have a responsibility to serve the Body of Christ first. Also, God has blessed you with opportunities that others do not have. And if you're not convinced this will work, our church will make sure that whoever you hire from us will be held accountable to do a good job for you!"

So the Christian businessman agreed to try the idea. He hired twenty people from our church, many of whom would be considered impoverished. We provided them with transportation to and from work until they could afford their own. We held them accountable for arriving at work on time and putting in a fair day's work for a fair day's wage. To further strengthen the accountability of these employees to the church, the businessman paid their salary to the church, which in turn paid the employees.

The employer was so impressed with the success of the program that he permanently hired seventeen of the first twenty employees. The program expanded, and in a six-month period our church placed fifty people. Today our church networks with other suburban Christian businessmen whom we have challenged to become involved.

Many churches must go one step further by actually creating opportunities for job development. This can be done through the creation of subsidiary businesses owned by the church. Deliverance Church in Philadelphia, for example, has developed a retail center that helps meet the needs of the community, provides jobs, and funds some of the church's outreach.

Churches can also help their members establish businesses by encouraging other members to do business with them. Ladies with secretarial skills, for example, can work out of their homes to meet the secretarial needs of individual church members as well as the corporate church.

Toward this end, our church has developed a business directory so that the members will know who in the body possesses the skills and services they may need. This type of networking allows the church to support the building of businesses, which in turn should provide more job opportunities for those within the church. Each person listed in the directory, however, must agree to church resolution of any conflicts between themselves and other members. Remember, benefits from the church require accountability to the church.

When the body of Christ addresses unemployment problems by finding jobs for everyone in the church who wants to work, many other problems are solved too. Poverty and homelessness are lessened. Financial crises facing families can be reversed. Dignity can be regained. Poverty can be replaced by productivity. The beautiful thing is, these things can be done through the church.

### THE CHURCH CAN TEACH JOB SKILLS

Obviously, the more skilled a person is, the better job he or she can obtain and the more money he or she can make. Not everyone who is poor has the ability to support himself. So it's important that the church also provide people with the opportunity to develop skills that will enable them to better provide for themselves. The church is well-suited to serve as an educational and training center in the community.

People who have valuable skills that they can teach to others can be found in most churches. If the church simply sets up a place and opportunity for people to develop new skills, they can become more employable. The Park Avenue Church of Minneapolis, Minnesota, has developed a highly technical skill-development program targeted at getting youth off the street and making them employable. Our church has now developed a "skills bank," primarily based on computer technology, that enables those without skills to learn skills that will enable them to increase their earnings. Using ten computers, people from the church who have computer skills volunteer their time to teach others to help themselves. We also have two bank-proofing machines and in about a month's time can train a person in this highly employable skill.

In addition, the church can help its members and other people in the community obtain a high school diploma. It's critical that people in our society learn how to read, write, and do basic math. Those who are illiterate have little opportunity to become productive, self-supporting members of society. So members in the church who have teaching credentials can become tutors and provide GED training. As people learn to read, write, and do math, they build a frame of reference that will help them develop greater skills in the future. For churches that really want to make a difference, the skill development possibilities are endless.

No matter how good the church's job training program may be, however, it will fail if it doesn't also develop moral integrity. It matters little that a person can do a job if he or she is not dependable, honest, or diligent. This is especially important when the training is provided by the church, which is to model God's image in the world.

To provide moral development along with skill development, the church's training program must include biblical training on integrity in the marketplace. Through this course we teach people the value of time, what it means to work for the glory of God, what it means to be faithful to Him, and what it means to know God personally. All of this training takes place within the context of solving a societal problem.

The process of meeting social needs through biblical solutions is not difficult or complex; it's available to the church if we just take the initiative to do it. If the church is going to lead the way in setting the agenda for addressing the problems of poverty and unemployment, we must do so from a biblical perspective. Our governing principle must be that poverty is best overcome by productivity. As the well-known axiom says, "If you give a man a fish, you feed him for a day. If you teach him to fish, you feed him for a lifetime."

# 15

# The Church and the Family

A single mother was having great problems with her rebellious son. He wouldn't obey her and was becoming involved in mischief, which if unchecked could lead to a life of crime. She came to the church for help because the church practices accountability. Five deacons visited the young man and let him know that if he continued to rebel, he would have to deal with them.

The young man was so shaken by their visit that he agreed to respect and obey his mother. But the deacons' responsibility did not stop with the young man's promise. They held that young man accountable to his commitment. They required him to call his assigned deacon every night when he came home. The assigned deacon also kept in touch with the mother to confirm that the young man was doing his homework and housework and was honoring her.

Today that young man is doing well. His mother sees a dramatic change in every part of his life. He is even telling his friends how the church kept him from going down the wrong road. The community is seeing what kind of difference the church can make.

This is what can happen when the people of God respond biblically to family problems. Men in the church were willing to be surrogate fathers and require a young man to function properly in his family. That's the kind of surrogate family presence the church needs to have today. That's what it will take to reverse the downward trend and save our young people.

## THE SPIRITUAL FUNCTION OF FAMILIES

God created the family to be the primary social institution through which moral values are transferred. But in our culture today, the family is no longer the central hub of society. Families are breaking up and are being restructured by divorce and remarriage. Secular thought and practices continually undermine parental responsibility and authority. Unless we can reestablish a family structure that is capable of transferring biblical moral values, our society will continue its downward spiral.

We must recognize that an inseparable link exists between God and family, family and church, and church and society. When we exclude God from the family, everything else suffers—in the family and in society. By contrast, when God is the center point of the family, there is hope for everything the family touches (which is everything).

The apostle Paul emphasized the relationship between family and society in his discussion of the link between the husband/wife relationship and the believer/church relationship (Ephesians 5:22-32). In fact, Paul concluded his lengthy discussion on how a husband and wife are to treat each other with the words, "I am speaking with reference to Christ and the church" (v. 32). He is saying that a proper *family* relationship is directly linked to a proper *spiritual* relationship.

Later, Paul tells children to obey their parents (Ephesians 6:1-3), concluding with the Old Testament promise "that it may be well with you, and that you may live long on the earth." Children who obey their parents have a respect for the family and a fear of God; they are quality people who cannot help but make a positive impact on society. Making an impact on society is part of God's purpose for the family.

Genesis tells us that God put man on the earth to have dominion over it and gave Eve to Adam to assist him in establishing dominion. To continue that dominion, God told them to be fruitful and multiply (Genesis 1:28). God created families to accomplish His purpose. God wants His image to be demonstrated throughout the world. When God's people train their children in His ways, His image is transferred from generation to generation, and the evidence of His glory can be seen throughout the earth.

Thus, the family is the place to raise children so that they can eventually leave home and continue the work of reflecting God in new places. Raising children biblically means providing a framework in which they can grow, be taught, and be disciplined. Home is where children learn how to live and fulfill their God-given responsibilities. Home is where children learn how they will influence society in positive, biblical ways.

We need to realize that the family is a covenantal entity. Malachi 2:14 says, "The Lord has been a witness between you and the wife of your youth, against whom you have dealt treacherously, though she is your companion and *your wife by covenant*" (italics added). For the family to fulfill its role of training and make a divine impact in history, it must abide by the authority structure God has established for it. This means that the husband is to operate under *God's* authority, the wife is to operate under her *husband's* authority, and the children are to operate under the *parents'* authority. A breakdown anywhere in the authority chain will result in the family's breakdown.

Part of the church's responsibility is to see that the marriage, and family, life of God's people is carried out according to His covenant. Therefore, it's legitimate for the church to get involved with a couple that's not getting along. It's legitimate for the church to assist parents in training their children in a biblical lifestyle. It's legitimate for the church to hold God's people accountable to God's covenants.

## KEEPING FAMILIES TOGETHER

The church needs to take definitive action to recapture the family for the glory of God. If we do not save the family, we have no hope of saving our nation. First and foremost, the church must set the agenda for keeping families together. By biblical standards, it ought to be impossible for church members to divorce without the church's knowing about it. It ought to be impossible for church members to have affairs and not be challenged by the church. It ought to be impossible for men in the church to neglect their responsibility as family providers.

Jesus made clear that no man, including the divorce court judge, has the right to separate what God has joined together. The church can grant divorces but only for the rare reasons of adultery or desertion. If the church doesn't grant a divorce, it isn't supposed to happen. However, we have allowed the world to set the agenda by granting so-called "no-fault" divorce, which is more accurately called "divorce on request." Singlehood is the only option for couples who separate without biblical grounds. If people really understood this, they'd work much harder at keeping their marriages strong.

If couples are struggling, the church should establish a biblical separation until the problems can be worked out (1 Corinthians 7:10-11). This includes determining who should move out of the home and how the children will be provided for. The church has the responsibility to oversee this process because marriage is a divine institution and the church represents God's authority. Couples who refuse to accept the involvement of the church are then subject to church discipline.

The biblical principles of separation and restoration in marriage work. I recently oversaw the separation of a couple in our church. Using biblical guidelines, we set the terms of the separation, provided counseling, established male and female support systems, and supervised help for the children. Today this couple can't thank the church enough for not allowing them to divorce. God is bigger than any marital crisis. It takes time and very hard work for the church to support marriages in crisis, but it is possible. The church must start showing the world how marriages work.

## HELPING SINGLE-PARENT FAMILIES

Another great area of need is financial and emotional support of single-parent families. God's intent is for families to have a father *and* a mother, not just a mother. Mothers can't be fathers; they can only be good mothers. A father brings a unique and necessary perspective to the home. In the father's absence, which is most often the case in single-parent homes, the men in the church ought to be fathering the fatherless. This is a major ministry opportunity that can show secular society how a successful extended family is supposed to work.

The church needs to provide Christian "big brothers" so that young men without fathers have a proper male image to imitate. There is no substitute for a young man's relationship with an adult male who provides a model of godly manhood. An adult man's commitment of quality time with a young man helps that young man establish biblical life priorities.

Additionally, the church can provide "fellowship families" in which a single-parent family unit has a dynamic relationship with a nuclear family unit. This will help single mothers and their children experience nuclear family relationships and provide them with a sense of belonging. These families can meet together for meals, family outings, and holidays. These times together will help build quality relationships in the church.

Churches can also help single mothers with day-to-day needs such as minor car repair and maintenance services. Men from one church I know of volunteer to do oil changes and the like on one Saturday a month.

Child care is another great need for both single-parent and two-parent families. The church can help by providing a safe environment for children when their parent(s) can't be at home. Church members can devote an hour or two a week to tutor children or help them with homework. This is especially helpful for single parents who don't have the support of a spouse to assist in their children's education. In addition, churches can provide child care for a "parents' day out" to give parents relief from child care and enable them to participate in activities that are important to their personal development.

## MODELING BIBLICAL SEXUALITY

The church also ought to lead the way in providing a renewed understanding of biblical sexuality. The church often expresses vehement dissatisfaction with secular society's sex education in which condoms replace morality. Yet in the church we barely talk about sex at all. It is imperative that we rise above our unbiblical sexual attitudes and teach our children about the nature, goal, purpose, and restrictions of sexual behavior. Our children need to know that sex is not just for personal gratification but is the expression and commitment of a lifetime of love.

The church needs to redefine manhood for young men so that manhood means more than sexual prowess. We must offer AIDS education classes. We must address the teen-pregnancy problem and the related physical, emotional, and financial consequences of abortion. We must faithfully support unmarried women and girls who are pregnant by offering classes in prenatal care, personal hygiene, and how to care for a baby. On a more personal level, the church can provide loving mentors who can teach and support unmarried, pregnant women in developing a moral lifestyle.

## OTHER ASSISTANCE

The church can also provide many services that Christian people have traditionally sought outside the church. For instance, churches could do a great service by providing family financial counseling. Many people need to know biblical principles of finance. They need to learn how to get out of debt and stay out of debt. The church can also become a major agent in arranging adoptions, particularly in the minority community, which suffers from a lack of black parents for black children.

The church needs to strengthen its ministry to couples and families on all levels. Family relationships are in crisis. The church needs to teach God's people about the vital purpose of family relationships in God's plan. The church needs to teach that family relationships are based on love and that when those love relationships break down, it leads to the breakdown of the family. The church needs to support couples who are struggling to help restore their marital relationship and preserve the family relationship. The church needs to show couples how a failure to raise their children in the ways of the Lord contributes to the breakdown of the family. If the church can't even help its own families learn how to function as God intends, there is no hope for halting further family breakdown in society.

# 16

# The Church and Crime and Drugs

Jim, the son of a member of our church, had stolen $1,500 from his employer. He was caught and faced a sentence at the Juvenile Detention Center. That sentence would have cost taxpayers $15,000 a year. He also would have been thrust into the company of others who had committed much more violent crimes and perhaps would have encouraged Jim to continue down the wrong road.

Instead, Jim received a sentence that changed his life. On the day he was to be sentenced, men from our church offered the judge another option. They explained that our church would provide this young man with a job and a male mentor who would teach him skills and responsibility, and that we would garnish his wages to pay back his former employer. We explained that we would hold Jim accountable and believed that within six months we could return to society a young man who would make a contribution to society rather than continue to be a burden.

Amazed at the support of the church, the judge gladly awarded Jim to our care. Today Jim's debt to his former employer is fully paid. He has a dynamic marriage, is the father of two lovely children, and is active in several ministries of the church.

That's just one illustration of what the church can do for society when it practices biblical social action. As a result of Jim's success, our church has been requested to repeat the process with twenty more young men from the Juvenile Detention Center. Why have we been allowed to do this? Because our justice system doesn't know what to do. The justice system knows it can't build enough prisons to house every offender. It knows that when people are released from prison they often continue to commit crimes. So when the justice system sees that the church can not only keep people out of prison but can also keep them from crime, the system will accept all the help it can get.

To arrive at long-term solutions to the problem of crime, we need to discover what God says about crime. Once we develop a biblical position on crime, we can begin to deal with the spiritual realities behind the problem and develop solutions to crime's overwhelming burden.

### A BIBLICAL PERSPECTIVE
### ON CRIME AND PUNISHMENT

In God's system of justice, there are no prisons. He established cities of refuge where those who committed accidental crimes would be protected from revenge, but He established no prisons. In God's system, people who do wrong are not locked out of society; they are required to make restitution for their crimes. In the case of capital crimes, where restitution is not possible, capital punishment was mandated.

Capital punishment is an emotionally charged issue. It is closely linked with the issue of justice and how fairly capital punishment is enforced. Admittedly there are serious inequities in the administration of capital punishment in our country. Therefore, Christians must aggressively pursue and promote the fair and consistent implementation of capital punishment. However, let's put these issues aside for a moment and focus on what God says about capital punishment.

After the Flood, God established a new covenant with Noah and his family. God told them how to live. He specified what was acceptable and what was forbidden. Since Noah was the father of the new human race (everyone else had been destroyed in the Flood), these instructions still apply. In the New Testament, Paul affirms the application of capital punishment when he says that the government wields the sword, the instrument of capital punishment (Romans 13:4).

Genesis 9:6 presents the use of capital punishment: "Whoever sheds man's blood, by man his blood shall be shed, for in the image of God He made man." In the Mosaic law, God gave specific guidelines for enforcing capital punishment. When addressing Noah's family, however, He merely indicated that death is the penalty for killing a person.

God requires such a severe punishment for murder because man is created in God's image. Man bears the mark of God and possesses a spiritual nature. Therefore, killing a man is a personal assault on God. At its foundation, capital punishment is a theological issue that relates to the very nature of God and man.

Jesus clarifies the proper perspective on capital punishment. In John 8 the Pharisees bring the adulterous woman to Jesus and ask if she should be killed. Contrary to what some people teach, Jesus recognized the legitimacy of capital punishment in this instance. He did not reject it. In fact, He endorsed it but with an important qualification. That qualification is that capital punishment be exercised justly by those who are not guilty of the same crime (Matthew 7:1-5).

The woman's accusers clearly were not interested in divine justice. They caught her in the act of adultery but only brought her to Jesus for judgment. They did not bring the man, although the law required that he be put to death also (Leviticus 20:10). They were promoting a double standard of which they themselves were guilty (John 8:7-9). Jesus' response to this incident indicates that justice must prevail in issues of capital punishment and that such punishment must be dispensed by qualified people.

Even when He stood before Pilate, Jesus recognized the legitimacy of capital punishment. He recognized that God had given Pilate power over life and death: "You would have no authority over Me, unless it had been given you from above; for this reason he who delivered Me up to you has the greater sin." (John 19:11). Jesus recognized the government's legitimate power to institute capital punishment.

We need to understand why God provided capital punishment. God demands righteousness, but man is depraved. God needs some way of reining man in so he can't relentlessly perpetuate evil. Therefore, He provided laws to maintain His righteousness in society. He also ordained governments to enforce those laws, which are designed to make people responsible. Laws provide appropriate standards for restitution and, in situations where that is not possible, capital punishment. God knew that His laws would be ignored, so part of His intention in mandating capital punishment was to create a deterrent against sin. If a person knows beyond any doubt that a particular action will result in certain death, that person will think twice about doing it.

Unfortunately, our system of capital punishment is rarely applied. Thus, it has lost its effectiveness as a deterrent to crime. For example, in 1933, the peak year for capital punishment in the United States, only 2 percent of the convicted murderers were put to death. That's not much of a deterrent. If the tables were turned and only 2 percent lived and 98 percent died—then a strong deterrent would exist.

Exodus 22:5-15 clearly sets forth the principle of restitution. Simply stated, the principle was that people must be held accountable to pay back the injured party for the losses incurred. This included restitution for stolen property (vv. 5, 7) and property damage (vv. 5-6, 14). Since much crime today deals with the area of theft and property damage, it seems that this principle would certainly be more effective than our society's current way of dealing with those crimes.

In our nation today, restitution is not practiced. We merely lock up criminals and give them free health and dental care, a warm bed, and food. Criminals in our society are barely inconvenienced, while society bears the burden of caring for them. Restitution, however, forces the criminal to learn responsibility. It causes the criminal to give something back to society, not just continue to take from society. Restitution inconveniences the criminal and protects the rights of the victim.

Crucial to the restitution process is the fact that restitution was determined by the judges. That is, the process was overseen legally, thus assuring accountability. That's where the church comes in. Paul says that the church is to have its own legal court system that deals with these matters: "Does any one of you, when he has a case against his neighbor, dare to go to law before the unrighteous, and not before the saints?" (1 Corinthians 6:1). He then raises the question, "Are you not competent to constitute the smallest law courts?" (v. 2). This responsibility includes everything related to this life (v. 3). To put it bluntly, Paul is saying that the secular courts should be learning how to practice law and exercise punishment from the church.

In the church I pastor in Dallas, we have a justice process that renders decisions on everything from restitution, as in Jim's case, to marital disputes, divorces, business lawsuits, juvenile delinquency, and so on. Of course, capital crimes fall solely under the jurisdiction of the state (Romans 13:1-4).

The church is not fulfilling its ordained role unless it serves as its own legal entity. Failure to submit to the final decisions of the church should mean excommunication from the church. Then and only then is the state to become involved. Because God's people have failed to sit as judges, the state does not see a model of divine justice at work. Therefore, it can't learn how to function properly. To remedy the situation, elders and deacons in the church must take up their rightful role as judges, and church members must be taught to submit to their biblical authority.

## THE CHURCH, THE GOVERNMENT, AND CRIME

The only way to successfully address the ever-increasing growth in crime is for the church to provoke the state to fulfill its divine mandate as the minister of God to be a terror to the unrighteous and to give praise to those who do good (Romans 13:1-3). Through the training of godly political leaders and the support of righteous laws that punish the evil and reward the good, the church should be the major influencing force in society's battle against crime. In fact, if the church were to influence the state to spend as much time and money to reward the good people as it presently uses to punish evil people, there could be a major reduction in the crime rate almost overnight.

For example, suppose people living in the inner city knew that they could get a down payment on a house for turning in a drug pusher; there would then be an incentive to fight crime. Our governments recognize the need for this type of activity on the part of citizens, which is why they allow "citizen's arrest." The problem is that it lacks incentive.

If the same economic incentives that pushers use to get kids to sell drugs were used to get people to report those who sell drugs, then teeth would be put into the biblical principle of "praising those who do good"; this most certainly means more than giving an occasional plaque to the citizen of the year.

Of course, there would have to be proper restraints so that vigilantism would not occur. These restraints would include having the appropriate authorities confirm the actual arrest and insisting that seizures be of a nonviolent nature. Also, fraud would have to be curtailed. A simple way this could be done would be that the person bearing false witness would be subject to a punishment similar to the one the accused would have received (Deuteronomy 19:16-21). Such a program would keep criminals off balance, since everyone in the community would be deputized to apprehend them. If the church took the lead in such activities, it would become the visible supporter of the state without infringing on the jurisdiction of the state.

## ADDRESSING THE SPIRITUAL REALITIES OF CRIME

Before devising any social action plan regarding crime, the church has to consider the spiritual realities that lead to crime. One of these spiritual realities is the family breakdown and the resulting breakdown of personal accountability.

We saw earlier that gangs have become surrogate families for many young people. The church can provide an alternative accountability structure that guides young people toward moral living. The church can create alternative "gangs," traditionally known as youth ministries, to get kids off the street and into constructive activities. To accomplish this successfully, young people should be broken down into smaller groups, based on age and sex, and have adult mentors who pour their lives into them. Older youth should be paired with younger ones to provide positive mentoring and peer pressure, which in turn helps the older youth learn responsibility.

Youth groups need to be more than entertaining gatherings. They need to become places of personal and spiritual development. Church buildings can be open at night, so kids can participate in games, movies, and discussions under adult supervision. By motivating God's people to commit the time to be models of influence in young people's lives, we can begin building a context for living that prevents young people from being influenced by those who would lead them down the road to destruction.

Crime is also motivated by drug involvement. In fact, our culture is in peril because of the rampant abuse of drugs. The use of drugs, itself a criminal activity, consumes vital resources and eventually leads to additional criminal activity to support the drug habit.

Drugs are fostered by two spiritual realities that make the problem almost insurmountable. First, greed—the desire to make money no matter what the price—plays a key role. The profit margin in drugs is phenomenal. It's easy to make a lot of money selling drugs. A teenager can work full-time at a fast food restaurant for a few dollars an hour, making at best $160 per week. But that same teenager can sell crack cocaine for only a few hours a day and easily make $500 or more in a week. So unless kids have strong spiritual and moral convictions, they're going to make the easy money. Staying in school has little significance for the drug pusher; his job doesn't require a high school diploma.

The second spiritual reality that makes drugs difficult to deal with is need—the individual's inability to control the passions of the flesh. Drug use may seem innocent enough at the beginning, but the need for it grows until its cravings exercise total control over a person. Drug use accomplishes one of two things for the user. It is a source of pleasure, or it provides an escape from reality. This latter need is generally generated by low self-esteem.

If we are going to address the problem of drug use, we need to stand with people and help them learn self-control. We can't just tell drug users to stop using drugs. If they are saying no to drugs, they need to be saying yes to something else. We can provide something to say yes to through the establishment of antidrug support groups. As Solomon said, two are better than one because they can protect, assist, and support each other (Ecclesiastes 4:9-12). As they hold each other accountable, they can help each other address and resist the temptation of drugs.

To help a person get off drugs, we have to walk with that person and lead him into a new environment. Why should a kid who is locked into poverty and sees no way out "just say no"? Why should a mother of four who knows she'll never be able to get off welfare "just say no"? It will take more than slogans to solve the drug problem; it will take a new frame of reference. We need to have a discipleship process going on.

We need to be available to hold people accountable to a biblical lifestyle and stand ready to pick them up when they fall. We need to provide regular support that encourages those who are struggling for deliverance from drugs. Then there is hope that people can participate in life without falling prey to the influences that led them into drugs in the first place.

The church can also serve as an educational center against drugs. Secular groups conduct drug education, but they don't necessarily provide the biblical, moral framework that is essential to keeping people off drugs. They most certainly do not offer the supernatural provision of the Spirit who guarantees victory over the desires of the flesh for all those who learn to walk in the Spirit (Galatians 3:16). This perspective is unique to the church. We must teach our children why drugs are evil. We must teach them what God says about drug use. We must teach them about the consequences of drug use. We must teach people to use spiritual resources to overcome drug habits.

Finally, we can use our churches to house programs designed to keep young offenders from continuing a life of crime. The church can offer tutoring and skill development so young people can overcome areas of deficiency and become gainfully employed. The church can offer peer counseling so people have Christian models who have overcome similar circumstances. The church can offer mentors so people are held accountable to make progress. The church can offer professional counseling so people can overcome deep-rooted problems.

These and other activities help people see their personal value and give them hope that they can make a positive contribution. A potential criminal needs to see that the rewards of obedience far outweigh the rewards of crime. Those rewards must go beyond simple dollars and cents; they must also be in terms of dignity, meaningful relationships, and quality of life. When the church responds biblically to the challenge, we will begin to see our society look to the church for answers.

# 17

# The Church and Discrimination

The apostle Peter was a committed Jew. He was born a Jew, bred a Jew, raised a Jew, and he was proud of it. Peter was so much a Jew that God had to get his attention through a vision to get him to even consider that, under the new covenant, Gentiles could be equal participants in God's family (Acts 10:10-17).

Because of that vision, Peter had to cross cultural, racial, and class lines. At first he did quite well, even eating with the Gentiles, which he never would have done before (Galatians 2:12). Everything went well until some influential Christian leaders showed up—who just happened to also be Jews. Suddenly Peter wasn't the man he had been. He "began to withdraw and hold himself aloof, fearing the party of the circumcision. And the rest of the Jews joined him in hypocrisy . . . even Barnabas" (Galatians 2:12-13).

What did Peter do? He based a decision about his behavior on culture rather than theology. He allowed cultural issues to dictate his decision, which had serious repercussions. When Peter, a leader in the church, made his move, everyone else followed—even Barnabas, who was the most Gentile-oriented man in the group. That discriminatory behavior might have been allowed to continue if it hadn't been for the intervention of Paul, another Christian Jew.

Before his conversion, Paul had been the perfect Jew; he was even a Pharisee. Yet as proud as Paul was of his Jewish heritage, he put it aside when he met Jesus. When Paul witnessed Peter's anticultural, racist behavior, he was compelled to put a stop to it. He stood before all of them and confronted Peter, declaring that such behavior was not of the gospel of Jesus Christ.

When Paul "saw that they were not straightforward about the truth of the gospel" (Galatians 2:14), he had to respond. He didn't act on the basis of popularity or emotions but on truth. That's what God's people must return to today.

The gospel proclaims that when people come to Jesus, their cultural, racial, and class barriers are superseded by loyalty to God's family. Cultures don't change. Races don't change. Economic status doesn't change. God doesn't want Jews to be Gentiles. He doesn't want whites to be blacks or blacks to be Hispanics. He created us to be different but to be one in the family of Christ. However, living by this truth isn't easy.

There is a distinction between *prejudice* and *discrimination*. Prejudice is our personal, inner bias against another person. Although that bias is sin, it is a matter of one's heart and often cannot be detected by another person. Discrimination, however, turns a bias in the heart into action against another person. Discrimination is visible; it is acting out ill feelings toward a group of people by treating them as inferior.

## PREJUDICE AND DISCRIMINATION IN THE CHURCH

It's ironic that our nation, which prides itself on being a "melting pot" of cultures, should be unable to bring people from different racial backgrounds together—particularly black and white—to function in harmony. It's tragic that God's people, who ought to be models of cultural harmony, haven't been able to overcome racial barriers either. We can safely say that 11:00 to noon on Sunday morning is the most segregated hour of the week in America. Christians of different backgrounds effectively separate themselves to worship the same God. The problem is not that people worship culturally but that such worship often reflects an unbiblical attitude.

During my early days at Dallas Seminary, my wife and I attended a prominent church in the area. The congregation sang "To God Be the Glory," but it was made known to us that blacks weren't welcome in that church. Of course, discrimination is a two-way street. People of different backgrounds and cultures sometimes do not feel welcomed in a minority church either.

Recently, an increased number of whites have begun attending our church in Dallas. One of the men in the church began to feel disturbed about this trend and asked what I was going to do about it. "Why not let them come?" I responded. He disagreed with me, fearing that too many whites would change the nature of our church. I told him, "Then you had better get busy and win blacks to Christ so we'll not be outnumbered." To have discouraged white participation in our church would have only been to repeat my negative experience with someone else.

In either case, discrimination in the church is wrong. The Bible is not silent about how we are to treat people who are different from us. The Bible says discrimination is evil. It is sin. Until we, as God's people, deal with racial, cultural, and class issues within the church, the church has nothing to offer the world in terms of solutions to racial problems. We must judge ourselves first so we can effectively judge society.

## A BIBLICAL VIEW OF DISCRIMINATION

The church, which attracts people from all walks of life and brings them together under the authority of Christ, has always had potential for prejudice and discrimination. Whenever you bring people of different economic status, different personalities, and different cultures together, the potential for prejudice, discrimination, partiality, or favoritism becomes a threat. The book of James provides a perspective on discrimination or favoritism in the church.

James begins his book by talking about the nature of the Christian faith. He sums up by saying, "This is pure and undefiled religion in the sight of our God and Father, to visit orphans and widows in their distress, and to keep oneself unstained by the world" (James 1:27). James doesn't care about stained-glass windows, plush carpet, or pretty choir robes. He cares about what God's people do; he cares about faith in action.

Within that context, James gets right to the point:

> My brethren, do not hold your faith in our glorious Lord Jesus Christ with an attitude of personal favoritism. For if a man comes into your assembly with a gold ring and dressed in fine clothes, and there also comes in a poor man in dirty clothes, and you pay special attention to the one who is wearing the fine clothes, and say, "You sit here in a good place," and you say to the poor man, "You stand over there, or sit down by my footstool," have you not made distinctions among yourselves, and become judges with evil motives? (James 2:1-4)

Essentially, James is saying that it's impossible to love God and have an attitude of personal favoritism. Personal favoritism means we look at a person on the outside and make a judgment about that person's value. It means we decide how to treat people according to inappropriate criteria—by cultural or economic standards rather than biblical standards.

Just to make sure we understand what he is talking about, James gives us an illustration of what personal favoritism, or discrimination, looks like. His illustration is equally valid today. When a wealthy man walks into the church wearing fancy clothes, we notice. We start calculating how much the offering will increase and how much more influence the church will have in the community because of this person's contacts, and we treat him right.

When a poor man walks in, wearing unfashionable, musty-smelling clothes, we write him off. We view him as just another drain on the ministry and hide him in the back row. In other words, we look at the outward appearance, judge the person's value to the church, and treat the person accordingly.

James analyzes the situation and essentially says to the church, "You discriminate when you do this! You talk about Jesus' love while you judge one another unjustly!" His message is that Christians ought not to discriminate on the basis of externals. The only valid distinctions are those made on the basis of biblical truth—not personality, money, or race.

Yet the church today often makes distinctions on the basis of cultural norms. We have made it more important to be culturally related than spiritually related. We have made it more important to be economically related than spiritually related. And until we become more concerned about doing what is right rather than taking sides, we will not overcome partiality in the church. Of course we ought to be culturally concerned, but cultural values must never dictate our spiritual values. Spiritual values must always take precedence.

What is the proper way for God's people to view others? James says it is with an attitude of love (James 2:8). Love supersedes all other laws governing human relationships. Love means that I have your best interest in mind. *Discrimination* means I have me in mind. *Classism* means I have me in mind. *Racism* means I have me in mind. God calls us to love our brother, not measure ourselves against him.

Finally, James says that God views partiality in the church as sin. He didn't say partiality is permissible because it's our personal preference or because it's how we were taught as children. James says that showing partiality is *sin* (James 2:9). Partiality of any kind—be it based on personality, race, or economic status—is wrong and results in God's judgment. This doesn't mean that everyone in the family of God is our best friend. We still have our differences. However, it means that everyone in God's family is to be treated with dignity and respect because of our common relationship in Christ.

In addition to James' clear teaching, Jesus' ministry provides us with an example of stretching beyond one's cultural boundaries. In John 4 we read about Jesus' remarkable encounter with a Samaritan woman. To understand the significance of this encounter, we must realize that vehement hatred, perpetuated for centuries, existed between the Jews and Samaritans. In fact, most orthodox Jews wouldn't even go into Samaria. However, Jesus went there intentionally to do His spiritual work.

Jesus knew that there was great spiritual need in Samaria, so He went out of His way—taking a great cultural risk—to meet that spiritual need. Jesus took the risk, sat down, and spoke with a Samaritan woman. Through their unusual conversation, the woman realized that Jesus was the Messiah, and many Samaritans believed in Him because of her testimony. Jesus' action clearly demonstrates that cultural differences must be subservient to the spiritual needs of others. Cultural barriers are no excuse for not communicating spiritual truth.

## PRACTICAL WAYS TO OVERCOME PREJUDICE

The time is long overdue for us to stop the foolishness of racism, classism, and culturalism in the church. We are all equal in the family of God. Our goal is not to establish a homogenized church, where everyone is the same in personality, economic status, or race. Rather, our goal is to establish a church where everyone of any race or status who walks through the door is loved and respected as part of God's creation and family. Let's look at what we can do to halt the tragedy of prejudice and discrimination among God's people.

The first step is for pastors to strive for biblical rather than cultural preaching. They must teach passages such as James 2 and Galatians 2 in light of their application to life today. Pastors must call discrimination of any kind by its rightful name—sin. We must be taught that our brothers and sisters in Christ are closer to us than our cultural or racial brothers and sisters and that our failure to love others in the family of God is an indictment on our relationship with God. Black is only beautiful if it is biblical, and white is only right if it agrees with the Holy Writ.

Pastors and church leaders must confront prejudice and discrimination more directly in ways that reflect the depth of pain that those attitudes cause. This includes confronting people when they demonstrate bias and exercising church discipline against those who persist in overt acts of discrimination. Churches that do not allow people to join because of race should not be allowed to remain part of the denomination. Leaders who can't accept people of different backgrounds in the church must be relieved of their duties, since those duties include caring for the entire flock.

Those who have been oppressed must also be willing to forgive those who genuinely seek forgiveness and not institute a process of reverse discrimination. Toward this effort, pastors must proclaim the theme of reconciliation, for reverse prejudice is no better than the prejudice that spawned it.

In order to counter cross-cultural stereotypes perpetuated by society, churches need to encourage cross-cultural exposure. This can start with an exchange of cultural and worship experiences between churches. Such exposure will help break down the walls of mistrust and prejudice. Several years ago, our church began such an exchange with a predominantly white North Dallas church. That experience has led to other areas of cooperation and mutual ministry. In fact, we work together to assist churches with fewer resources.

Although God doesn't demand that all churches integrate, He does demand that churches work together to build His kingdom. When churches network together, they have potential to make maximum impact on society. For example, churches can cooperate in evangelistic outreaches and social service projects as well as in sharing resources and skills.

Furthermore, churches can join together in speaking out to the broader society against prejudice and other social issues. Society needs to know where the church stands. It is important that the church be heard as a unified voice in arenas of influence. Our failure to speak out corporately and publicly keeps the church in the background and prevents it from becoming the powerful influence in society that it ought to be.

Christians need to begin identifying our common ground with one another. This was Jesus' strategy with the Samaritan woman. Since both the Jews and Samaritans considered Jacob to be their father, Jesus met her at Jacob's Well—a place of mutual agreement, which was the starting point of their relationship.

This means that, rather than starting with the problems we face cross-culturally or cross-racially, we need to start with the areas of greatest strengths or commonality. Many business deals are cut on the golf course, tennis court, or over lunch because such settings give a context of commonality. Both blacks and whites, rich and poor, need to join forces on issues of mutual interest. One time we may join together against abortion, another time against apartheid. On other occasions we may join forces on issues that are neutral but necessary for the kingdom, such as serving together on community boards, chambers of commerce, boards of education, or even joint venturing on a Christian school project.

When we are fighting a war, the color, class, or culture of the man fighting next to you doesn't matter as long as he is fighting on your side. The church is fighting the same enemy, yet we have been so busy fighting each other that we haven't accomplished much. All Satan has to do to defeat us is to simply encourage us to continue doing what we are already doing—destroying each other rather than attacking him (James 4:1-2).

The church plays a vital role in society. We are responsible to build up God's kingdom and demonstrate His glory to the world. We are to continually reach out—beyond our comfort zones—to meet the spiritual needs of our society. We cannot accomplish our task when we are encumbered by any kind of discrimination. It is imperative that we build up one another—regardless of our cultural, economic, or racial differences—and make a comprehensive spiritual impact on the world.

# 18

## Conclusion: Setting a New Agenda for Society

The true story is told of a world champion chess player who was visiting art galleries during his vacation in Europe. While touring one of the galleries, he came across a painting that stopped him in his tracks. It was a picture of a chess game.

On one side of the painting was the devil. He was laughing, excited, and full of joy. He was about to make his move. On the other side of the painting sat a young man whose face was filled with terror. He sat biting his fingernails, his knees were knocking, and sweat was pouring down his face. The chess champion understood the scenario when he saw the title of the painting. It was called *Checkmate*. The devil was about to make the final move to claim this young man's soul.

The chess champion was awestruck by the painting. He studied it for hours. Gradually a smile came across his face. A gleam twinkled in his eye as he asked for a chessboard. Upon receiving it, he set the board up precisely as it was in the painting.

After studying it for a while, he turned to the young man, as though he were alive and said excitedly, "Young man, I have some good news for you. Things are not as bad as they seem. Even though it looks like you've lost, there's still one more move left on the board. After the devil makes his move, you will get the final move."

That's the message of this book. America, despite the problems it faces, still has one more move, and it belongs to the church. But we must be willing to make that move. All the other moves have already been tried.

If we're ever going to take back our culture—stop the destruction of our children, our neighborhoods, our families, and our society—we must have a vision. We must see the move. If the church is ever going to set the agenda for society, rather than stumbling along and repeating the same failures as society, we must have a vision. If God's people are ever going to turn the world upside down by demonstrating God's image in every area of life, we must have a vision. We must have God's vision and live by it.

## VISION IS A WORD FROM GOD

Scripture says that without a vision, the people perish (Proverbs 29:18). It's safe to say that our society—and for the most part, even the church—is perishing. We desperately need a vision. In Hebrew, the word for vision means "prophetic revelation." So Scripture is saying that unless we have a revelation from God, we will perish. A vision, therefore, isn't something we make up or dream up; it is the Word of God.

Our communities today are perishing because there is little Word from God, little prophetic revelation from God at work in society. We have many preachers, but little Word. We have church buildings, but little Word. We have revivals, but little Word. To have a vision, we must have His Word; we must have His revelation in Scripture.

Our vision comes from God's Word, but it isn't a one-shot deal. We must go back to Scripture repeatedly and apply it to every part of life. When we apply God's revelation comprehensively to every part of life, we will have a vision. We will have a vision that touches every part of life and makes an impact on society.

One man with a vision was Nehemiah. Nehemiah had a good thing going. He was a cupbearer for the king, so he had a stable, good-paying job. The benefits weren't bad either. He was always in a comfortable environment—fit for a king—and was able to travel wherever the king traveled. Then Nehemiah heard that Jerusalem was in shambles and that the people were in great distress (Nehemiah 1:3).

When Nehemiah heard the news, he wept, for he knew that God no longer had a visible testimony in Israel, which meant no light for the rest of the world. So he prayed and fasted for days. Notice how Nehemiah's prayer began: "Remember the word which Thou didst command Thy servant Moses" (Nehemiah 1:8). This isn't a "Lord bless me" prayer. It is a prayer of vision. It is a prayer based on God's revelation applied to a life situation.

Through interaction with God's Word, Nehemiah received a vision. He was called to accomplish God's work. He received a revelation from God to rebuild the walls of Jerusalem, and he did it. We must remember that God's Word is the ultimate standard by which His people operate. God's Word is our vision.

## VISION HAS A PRICE

The job God gave to Nehemiah to accomplish wasn't easy. He paid a price to accomplish the work God had revealed to him. He had to leave his home and his good job. He had to travel through dangerous lands. He had to deal with difficult people, famine, and sin. Yet, because he was willing to make personal sacrifice, God's work was done.

Many Christians today don't want to pay the price of fulfilling God's vision. Jesus has already paid the price for our salvation, but we have been saved to fulfill God's Word in the world. We have been saved to make a difference, and making a difference will cost us something. We may need to put in some overtime to build the wall. We may need to cut back on our personal profits to build the wall. But build the wall we must.

Jesus said that if we are to be His followers, we must deny ourselves. That means we submit our lives—our goals and desires—to His lordship. It means that we are willing to set aside our goals to bring about His purpose in the world around us. It means we take risks.

Daniel was a man who was willing to take those risks. As a young man, Daniel was chosen by King Nebuchadnezzar to be trained for leadership in the Babylonian Empire (Daniel 1:5-7). This was a rare opportunity for an Israelite. It gave Daniel the opportunity to live in the king's house, eat the king's food, and become the king's top administrator. It offered all the power and luxury in the empire. It was a great improvement over slavery—Daniel's only other option.

However, Daniel knew God's Word and had made a commitment to live according to God's commands. One of those commands was not to eat meat offered to idols (Exodus 34:15). By being one of the king's chosen few, Daniel had a problem. The king's choice food, which Daniel was expected to eat, had been offered to the Babylonian idols. Daniel could not eat it and be true to God's Word. So at great personal risk, he politely asked Melzar, who was in charge of the training, for an exemption (Daniel 1:8-16).

Melzar at first protested. He knew the king would kill him if the young Israelite wasn't as healthy or intelligent as the other young men. Yet Daniel persisted and suggested a ten-day testing period in which he and his three Israelite friends would eat only vegetables and water. Melzar agreed to the test, and in ten days Daniel and his friends were healthier and wiser than all the others. By taking a risk, perhaps of life and death, Daniel and his friends began to establish a divine testimony before the king.

Later in his life, under the reign of King Darius, Daniel once again stood by God's vision (Daniel 6:1-26). Daniel had a high position and an impeccable record in the Persian Empire. Other officials were jealous and wanted Daniel out of power. Try as they might, they couldn't find anything personally or professionally to use against him. The only way they could get rid of Daniel was to pass a law against prayer to God.

Even though prayer to God was outlawed, Daniel continued to pray faithfully. He was caught in the act and sentenced to death in the lions' den. But even a death sentence could not prevent God from doing His work through Daniel. The lions didn't touch Daniel, and in the morning, King Darius learned that Daniel was still alive. At that moment, King Darius recognized Daniel's God. He decreed that everyone "tremble before the God of Daniel" (Daniel 6:26).

Daniel's faithfulness as a disciple impacted an entire nation. Because Daniel lived by God's standards and performed his duties well, he had the opportunity to appoint others to powerful positions. When the time came, he chose Shadrach, Meshach, and Abed-nego, his three friends who had also refused to eat the king's meat. Daniel used his power in the secular world to duplicate God's influence in high places. He knew that three more men who were committed to living by God's standards would have an even greater impact on society than he could have alone.

Because God had said, "You shall have no other gods before Me" (Exodus 20:3), the three men refused to bow and worship the image of King Nebuchadnezzar (Daniel 3:4-12). For their disobedience, they were sentenced to death in a fiery furnace. The furnace was so hot that it killed the soldiers who threw Shadrach, Meshach, and Abed-nego into it, but the three lived. They were such a powerful testimony to their God that Nebuchadnezzar decreed death to anyone who said anything offensive against Him (Daniel 3:27-29).

God's people have always had the ability to change the course of history. We see evidence of this in Genesis, where we read about Abraham and Lot and the destruction of the wicked cities Sodom and Gomorrah, and the life of the prophet Elijah who called on God to stop the rain because of a wicked queen. But God's people must make a decision to live by God's vision. When Jonah finally decided to follow God's vision, a whole nation was redeemed from death and destruction (Jonah 2:4-10).

Esther faced a decision of vision (Esther 4:11-14). She had to risk her safety and security in the king's court to accomplish God's plan. Realizing that her position as queen was theologically provided, not just humanly appointed, she made the right choice and delivered a whole nation from death.

Today God also needs disciples who will take the risk of standing with His Word against society's standards. Social programs, psychiatrists, and all the money in the world cannot reverse what is happening in our society. God doesn't use those things to accomplish His work unless they are based on His Word. God uses His people to apply His Word and make a difference in society. God uses His disciples who live by His vision.

The process of change in society starts with each one of us. We can't merely proclaim the answers to society; we must live them. We may think that by simply living as God's people, we aren't doing enough. That isn't true. The life of only one disciple, who lives all of life by God's standards, can change an entire nation.

## DISCIPLESHIP CAN CHANGE SOCIETY

The story of Nehemiah doesn't end with the completion of the wall. Rather, the completion of the wall began a remarkable revival in the whole society (Nehemiah 8:1-12). When the wall went up, the people suddenly became hungry for the Word of God. They called out for Ezra to read the Word to them. They listened to the Word for six hours straight. They didn't watch television for six hours. They didn't watch a ball game for six hours. They listened to God's Word for six hours. Why did they suddenly have such an intense desire for God's Word?

When the wall went up, the Israelites saw what the Word of God can do. They began to think, *Maybe God knows what He's talking about. Maybe Scripture is for real. If God can build this wall in fifty-two days, maybe He can help me straighten out my life.* They witnessed what God's Word can accomplish corporately and decided they wanted that in their lives too.

People today, although they may not know it, are hungry for a revelation from God. They know their relationships are messed up. They know the way they live is messed up. They know they don't really know how to make things right. So when God's people model the righteousness of God before them, when these people see how life as God intends it to be lived is lived, they will notice. They will be ready to receive the Word of God.

When people are presented with the Word of God, it makes a difference. As Ezra read the book of Genesis to the Israelites, they began to weep. They saw how far they were removed from God. They saw their own unrighteousness. They mourned over their sin. They changed their ways, and it all began because Nehemiah had a vision.

Nehemiah had a vision that he was willing to pay the price to live by. He was greatly inconvenienced and had to overcome many obstacles, but he made a difference for God. I like the fact that in just 52 days Nehemiah built a wall that had been destroyed for 150 years. That tells me that God wanted the wall rebuilt all along. All He waited for was someone who was willing to pay the price—someone who was willing to be a disciple He could use.

God is looking for that today. He is looking for disciples, people He can use, to accomplish His purpose in our world. God is looking for individuals who will say, "Yes, I'm going to be Christ's disciple. I will pay whatever price is necessary to be used for God's purposes."

It will take a collective movement of individual disciples to make the dramatic impact that needs to be made on our society. But a collective movement doesn't create itself; it is the result of individuals who make a commitment. We can talk about building a testimony for God all we want to, but until we make an individual decision to be Christ's disciples, we will have no impact.

In the movies and on television, previews show coming attractions. Designed to create interest, the previews always show the most dynamic and dramatic parts, such as the chase scenes, love scenes, and fight scenes. The whole point of the previews is to whet our appetites for the upcoming programs.

Someday a big show will come to town, and Jesus will be the star. It will be a worldwide performance, and the cast will be sensational. But until then, He has left previews of coming attractions in the world. He has left His church to provide clips of the major production that is to come.

Unfortunately, some of the clips are so bad that people have little interest in attending the major performance. The church has been so weak in demonstrating the power and wonder of the main feature that fewer and fewer people have interest in it.

It's time for God's people—the church—to start showing previews that are worth watching: previews to the world that will prompt the question, "Where can I buy a ticket for the show?" Then we can respond, "No purchase is necessary. We're giving the tickets away. The price has already been paid."

# A Personal Word

Dear Friend,

I hope this book was thought-provoking and gave you a deeper under-standing of the problems facing urban America. I hope it brought you closer to God and made a difference in your life.

More than anything, my friend, I hope it has challenged you and moved you to action. Right now you might be thinking, "Sure, I'd like to help, but what can one person do?"

Rosa Parks was just one person, yet she helped change forever the per-ception that a person should be relegated to the back seat because of the color of their skin. Henry Ford was just one person. You need only look on any traffic-filled street to see the impact he made on the world.

And the mother of Jesus Christ was just one person, one very human woman who obediently answered God's call to serve.

You see, change doesn't happen overnight. It begins with one person seeing a problem and making a conscious decision to make a difference, to become part of the solution.

I'd like to share with you four ways you can begin to make a difference in your life, your family, your city.

1. You can make a difference by caring about your family. By taking time for them. By bringing up your children in the church and giv-ing them a biblical outlook on life.
2. You can make a difference by caring about your neighbor. By giving food to the hungry, clothing to the needy, shelter to the homeless. You can make a difference by writing to government leaders, taking a stand for what is right and admonishing them to do the same. You can make a difference by being a role model to a young person in need of guidance.
3. You can make a difference by becoming an Urban Alternative min-istry partner. We're dedicated to strengthening the family and find-ing Scriptural solutions to every problem  faced by society today.
4. You can make a difference by praying. The most important thing you can do about any problem is pray. Pray for guidance, for understand-ing, for wisdom, for a heart moved to action. At The Urban Alter-native, prayer is our number one tool.

We receive letters daily from people sharing the difference prayer has made in their lives. We invite them, as I invite you now, to become prayer warriors for our embattled cities. I ask you to pray for The Urban alternative, for me, for our workers, for the thousands of pastors, church leaders, and men, women and young people across the country who are diligently working to bring about change through Jesus Christ and the Word of God.

I wrote this book because I'm a servant of God, and as such I'm dedicated to changing urban cities from the inside out. I believe the only way that will be accomplished is through people who are changed from the inside out.

One of the ways The Urban Alternative helps people change is through our radio ministry. We have both daily and weekly programs on stations across the country. Each program focuses on God's Word and how we can apply the word to our lives each day.

We also work with pastors, community leaders and others interested in helping their cities. The Urban Alternative offers a variety of conferences, training programs, cassettes, videotapes, books, and other information to help people reach their God-given potential.

Our goal is to give individuals and churches the tools and knowledge they need to make a difference in their own communities.

We need to get back to the basics, to family, to morality, to honesty, to integrity, to caring about our neighbors, to being involved.

Before taking any action, however, you need to make sure you are right with God.

God's Word, the Bible, is a blueprint for our lives. In it is found the answer to every single problem. When people stand up and are counted, things happen. The atmosphere changes. Hope is restored . . . one person, one family, one church, one city at a time.

And it can start with you.

If you would like information on how to become a child of God, or more information about The Urban Alternative, please write me.

I'd really like to hear from you. Here's my address:

Dr. Anthony T. Evans
The Urban Alternative
Post Office Box 4000
Dallas, TX 75208

God bless you as you choose to make a difference for yourself, your family, and your city. I hope to hear from you soon.

DR. ANTHONY T. EVANS